COLLECTOR'S
VALUE GUIDE™

The BOYDS COLLECTION LTD.

Boyds Plush
Animals

Secondary Market Price Guide
& Collector Handbook

FOURTH EDITION

The
BOYDS COLLECTION LTD.

This publication is not affiliated with The Boyds Collection Ltd.® or any of its affiliates, subsidiaries, distributors or representatives. Any opinions expressed are solely those of the authors, and do not necessarily reflect those of The Boyds Collection Ltd. "The Bearstone Collection®" and "The Folkstone Collection®" are registered trademarks of The Boyds Collection Ltd. "The Dollstone Collection™," "Yesterday's Child™," "The Shoe Box Bears™" and "DeskAnimals™" are trademarks of The Boyds Collection Ltd. Product names and product designs are the property of The Boyds Collection Ltd., Gettysburg, PA. Artwork used with permission.

Front cover: "Aunt Yvonne DuBeary"
Back cover (left to right): "Prudence Bearimore," "G. Kelly Ribbit," "Kerry Q. Hopgood," "Stevenson Q. Bearitage"

Managing Editor:	Jeff Mahony	Art Director:	Joe T. Nguyen
Associate Editors:	Melissa A. Bennett	Production Supervisor:	Scott Sierakowski
	Jan Cronan	Graphic Designers:	Lance Doyle
	Gia C. Manalio		Sean-Ryan Dudley
	Paula Stuckart		Kimberly Eastman
Contributing Editor:	Mike Micciulla		Ryan Falis
Editorial Assistants:	Jennifer Filipek		Jason C. Jasch
	Nicole LeGard Lenderking		David S. Maloney
	Ren Messina		David Ten Eyck
	Joan C. Wheal		
Research Assistants:	Priscilla Berthiaume		
	Beth Hackett		
	Steven Shinkaruk		

ISBN 1-888914-46-7

CheckerBee
PUBLISHING
(formerly Collectors' Publishing)
306 Industrial Park Road • Middletown, CT 06457

TABLE OF CONTENTS

TABLE OF CONTENTS

INTRODUCING THE COLLECTOR'S VALUE GUIDE™

*W*elcome to the Boyds Plush Animals Collector's Value Guide™! This is the first time we'll be focusing exclusively on those irresistible plush characters made by The Boyds Collection Ltd. and this expanded edition will give you all the great information that you've come to expect from the Collector's Value Guide and so much more!

A Little Bit Of Boyds

First, we'll give you a history of the Boyds line, telling you about how the line began, as well as a look at the plush series. Then we'll hear from Mary Beth Roe, the QVC Senior Program Host who appears with "The Head Bean Hisself" on the "Boyds Bears Show," in an exclusive interview. We'll also give you the latest updates on the line, including the new 1999 pieces and future retirements.

The Collector's Value Guide™

In this section, you'll find individual, full color photos of each piece, as well as all their relevant information, including item number, issue year, retirement status and 1999 secondary market value.

Special Features

The fun continues with a walk through the wilds of the secondary market and sections on variations and displays. All of this and more is available to you in the Collector's Value Guide™, your complete Boyds plush resource.

G ary Lowenthal, creative genius behind The Boyds Collection Ltd. began his career as an entrepreneur by running his own antiques shop, The Boyds Collection, in Maryland. Before long, however, he moved to Pennsylvania and formed a partnership with artist Gae Sharp that would change his life. In 1987, the two joined together to create a line of jointed teddy bears that would soon take the world by storm. Since then, The Boyds Collection Ltd. has expanded to include hares, cats, dogs and a wide array of other plush characters, as well as five successful resin lines; The Bearstone Collection®, The Folkstone Collection®, The Dollstone Collection™, The Shoe Box Bears™ and DeskAnimals™.

BEAR NAKED

Each season, Boyds debuts almost 100 new plush pieces and since the line's inception, there have been nearly 1,000 furry friends introduced, each belonging to one of the many Boyds series. Each animal has its own individual look that allows the Boyds "personality" to shine through. In addition to fur color and fabric differences, each piece has unique facial features as well. Top the whole thing off with creative and witty names and these animals really have flair!

Also adding to the allure of Boyds plush, many of the pieces in the collection come dressed to impress. Outfits may be as simple as a jaunty bow or as complex as an intricately sewn dress and matching hat. So, no matter whether you have simple tastes or prefer extravagantly dressed and accessorized bears, hears and more; you're sure to find more than a few friends to accompany you home from your favorite retail store.

WHILE SUPPLIES LAST

Since the early days, "Bailey" (named for the Head Bean's daughter) and her friends "Emily Babbit" and "Edmund" have become three of the most popular pieces in the collection. Ever since 1992, the three have been introduced twice a year (in the spring and fall) to model the hottest trends in fashion and charm collectors everywhere. In 1996, Bailey's brother "Matthew" joined the well-dressed clan, although he is only offered each fall, because, as the Head Bean explains, "by the time he gets around to him, G.M. is too pooped to design." And like any faithful pooch, Matt's dog "Indy" was not far behind him, joining the set in 1997. Each piece is retired after only one year of production to make room for the next collection of limited editions.

EXCLUSIVELY YOURS

In addition to their regular line of products, Boyds releases a wide range of exclusive pieces; which, each year, are offered through select retail outlets, be it a store, catalog or even on television. Today, QVC, the home shopping network, is one of the largest and most popular dealers of Boyds exclusives due, in part, by their ease-of-use. Exclusive pieces can often be hard to track down as they are released in limited quantities at a limited number of locations, so they often come and go before collectors even become aware of their existence.

ACCESSORIES MAKE THE BEAR

Do you know what your bears and hares do when you leave the house? To keep them out of trouble, Boyds has designed a wide variety of accessories for your furry friends to play with while you're gone. With options like playing "dress up" with the multitude of sweaters and dresses available, to learning to cook with their own bear-sized kitchen appliances, your animals will never be bored again. Also available is pint-sized furniture so that you can be sure that all your Boyds friends are as comfortable as possible in their new environment. And don't think for a second that the Head Bean left out his human friends; Boyds artwork can be found on everything from cookie jars to throws that are just as warm and cuddly as your stuffed companions. (For more information on Boyds plush accessories, see the *Boyds Plush Accessories* section beginning on page 205.)

ON THE ROAD

No look at the world of Boyds would be complete without a look at Gary Lowenthal, "The Head Bean Hisself." A collectible artist with celebrity status, Gary is well-known for his eccentric and outgoing personality. He is highly visible, often making appearances at hundreds of shows and shops during the year; always taking time to speak with each collector while signing their pieces. Pieces available on the Boyds Bears QVC specials, titled "The Mary Beth and Gary Show," often sell out immediately and have consistently been some of the channel's highest-rated shows. Opportunities to see Gary and "what he'll do next" have become as much a part of collecting Boyds as the lovable animals themselves.

*T*he lovely "Bailey" and friends, those coveted limited editions, have been delighting collectors since 1992 with their diverse wardrobe that includes everything from carefree denim jumpers to elegant velvet dresses. Each season, a theme is chosen for the collection and all the participants are perfectly attired to suit the occasion. Along with the regular limited editions, there has been an exclusive set offered each fall since 1996 featuring "Bailey" and "Matthew" and two matching resin ornaments. Here's a look at some of the popular themes featured so far:

SPRING 1995 – All decked out for a day at sea, "Bailey" and "Emily Babbit" sported navy and white dresses; while "Edmund" looked seaworthy in a sweater featuring an anchor design and a sailor hat.

SPRING 1996 – Dressed in their Sunday best, "Bailey" and "Emily Babbit" donned pastel-patterned cardigans, while "Edmund" was handsomely attired, although perhaps uncomfortable, in a checkered sweater and bowtie.

SPRING 1998 – This season saw nurses "Bailey" and "Emily Babbit" offering some tender loving care to "Edmund," who apparently got a bit too close to the beehive. The girls looked adorable in their off-white uniforms and "Edmund" looked sweet as honey in his sweater, appropriately with a beehive sewn on front.

FALL 1998 – Belle of the ball, Bailey and her consorts looked like royalty in elaborate velvet outfits. "Bailey" appeared in red, while "Emily Babbit" was in green and "Edmund" looked like a prince in a cream sweater. Completing the group, "Matthew" chose a green velvet jacket and burgundy pants and "Indy," the royal pooch, donned a plaid bandanna and a Santa hat.

*W*hile every plush animal is different in its own way, Boyds has grouped animals with similar characteristics into categories to make them easier to identify. Here's a brief description of each of the different series:

Animal Menagerie ... Just like the name implies, this is a collection of the less common animals in the collection. Donkeys, elephants, gorillas and pigs are just a sample of the animals you'll find in this category.

The Archive Series ... Designed in the style of the antique jointed teddy bear, several of these elegant animals are named after characters from merry old England.

The Artisan Series ... A showcase for new artists, this series features animals of all types by "up-and-coming" designers.

BabyBoyds ... Designed for younger Boyds collectors, these cuddly characters are "double bagged," meaning that if the bean stuffing bursts the inner lining (due to the wear and tear of little ones) there is another lining to prevent spills. *BabyBoyds* are created with a super soft fabric and are also poseable.

Bears In The Attic ... Perfect for hugging, these bears, hares and friends are made of sherpa pile and ultra-soft chenille. They were created to have the look of well-loved and long-lost toys from days gone by and are extremely durable.

The Bubba Bears ... These lovable bears come with moldable faces that can convey any expression that you want to give them! The last of *The Bubba Bears* retired in 1997.

The Choir Bears ... These saintly bears and hares are designed so they can sit, stand or kneel in prayer.

Clintons Cabinet ... Named after the president's family and some of his advisors, many of these pieces have already been retired.

Doodle Bears ... The smallest of the Boyds plush series, the *Doodle Bears* consists of three brightly colored bears, all named after famous political icons.

The Flatties ... These animals are the perfect companion for those lazy afternoons. Their favorite hobby is "just lying around" and they make great pillows!

Grizzly Bears ... At first impression, these leather-decorated bears look tough. But despite their rough and gruff appearance, these bears are really quite lovable once you get to know them.

Hares In Toyland ... One of the older plush series, these hares were all retired by 1995. They can be recognized by their extra tall stature and their ability to stand all by themselves.

Himalayan Dancing Bears ... A truly unique line of animals, these bears look like they've been stopped halfway through evolution. With long curved paws and hunched backs, these bears are a sight to see!

J.B. Bean & Associates ... Fully poseable, these bears, hares, cats, dogs and the like are filled with bean pellets. Together, these pieces make up the "elite" of the Boyds series.

The Mohair Bears ... Referred to by the Head Bean as "Upah Clahss, yet Affordable," most of these bears, hares and cats are limited to six months or one year of production. In 1999, several mini-*Mohairs* (4.5" tall) debuted and, unlike their larger cousins, are not limited. Many of the bears are named for U.S. Presidents; while many of the hares are named for First Ladies.

PLUSH SERIES – ANIMAL MENAGERIE TO WOOL BOYDS

Northern Lights... Made up of members of the Von Hindenmoose family, these moose have travelled a long way to join the rest of their Boyds family!

Prime Minister's Cabinet... The Canadian equivalent to *Clintons Cabinet*, these bears are named after past Prime Ministers and are exclusive to that region.

Snow Bears... Like their name implies, these bears of the Arctic are all white and often have irresistible blue eyes.

Squeekies... The animals in this series will talk back to you if squeezed just right!

T.F. Wuzzies... These bears are made out of heavy-duty fabric and resemble the delicate mini-bears that are on the market today – but at a less expensive price. While the bears are all 5" or less, they make a huge impression.

T.J.'s Best Dressed... The largest (and the most stylish) of the plush series; all of the characters in this category are no slouches in the fashion department.

Wool Boyds Series... This series is composed of members of the Von Bruin family. These German bears (and dog) have thick, wooly coats to protect them from the cold.

Ornaments... Although these pieces are perfect for the holiday tree, they are too adorable to be stored away after Christmas. Collectors can have a ball while coming up with display ideas for these miniature creatures.

*C*apitalizing on the success of his Boyds bears, creator Gary Lowenthal was inspired to replicate the plush in a line of "sculptural interpretations," better known as Boyds resin figurines. The collection, which debuted with The Bearstone Collection, has since grown to include The Folkstone Collection, The Dollstone Collection, The Shoe Box Bears and DeskAnimals.

THE BEARSTONE COLLECTION

Since its introduction in 1993, The Bearstone Collection has expanded to include a bevy of wonderfully detailed figurines, as well as a variety of ornaments, plaques, votive holders, waterglobes, musicals, frames, clocks and pins. The collection now consists of over 300 pieces. Included in The Bearstone Collection are two series, the *Holiday Pageant Series*, whose members will all face retirement in 1999, and *Noah's Pageant Series*, which makes its debut this year.

THE FOLKSTONE COLLECTION

In the folk art style of pencil figurines, The Folkstone Collection is a tall and thin assortment of personalities – from the angelic to the amphibious. The collection now totals over 250 pieces. Included in the Folkstones, is the *Carvers Choice* series, which is a collection of traditional folk art pieces with the look of hand-carved wood, while the *Santa & Friends* series features Santa both at work and at play. *The Wee Folkstones* are faeries, angels (in training), snowpeople, gnomes, elves, and other "wee companions." *Ribbit & Co.*, a series within *The Wee Folkstones*, is a set of frogs in search of kisses, flies and a good bottle of wine.

The Dollstone Collection

The main characters in this collection are children brought to life with the innocence of a bygone era. These smoothly finished pieces depicting "Yesterday's Child" were initially introduced to collectors in 1995 on QVC and, in 1996, they made their way to retail stores. This growing collection of over 80 pieces includes figurines, ornaments, musicals, porcelain dolls, votive holders and waterglobes.

The Shoe Box Bears

The Grizberg family of bears was introduced in 1996. This collection was appropriately named because Lowenthal, as a young boy, kept his toys and treasures in shoe boxes. There are now 15 Shoe Box animals in all (yes, there has even been a hare infiltration!). Adding to the allure of these lovable animals is their unique body style. All Shoe Box Bears have limbs that are connected to their bodies with rubber bands, which makes them poseable.

Desk Animals

The rather unusual DeskAnimals swam into the collection in 1998. These charming, multi-piece animals are designed to appear as if they are submerged underwater on their way to the other side of the river. Appealing to the wild side in all of us, the DeskAnimals include a variety of species which include a well-racked moose, a papa bear giving his cub a piggy-back ride and a hippopotamus with a mouth large enough to insert your business cards (well, almost!).

Inside
Boyds

*O*nce you enter the world of the Boyds Collection Ltd., you won't want to leave. There is something uniquely different about this collection; something that makes it different from other collectibles on the market. From the adorable bears, hares and assorted critters to the Head Bean Hisself, artist and creator Gary Lowenthal, everything about the The Boyds Collection Ltd. is often just a little left of center.

INQUIRING MINDS WANT TO KNOW!

Each of the characters in the collection possesses a charming lightheartedness, which is directly inherited from The Head Bean, Gary Lowenthal. Who else could come up with a life-like Boston Terrier named "Philo Puddlemaker?" Collectors can delve into the mind of the wacky artist by reading his company newsletter, "The Boyds Retail Inquirer." The bulletin is written by the Head Bean Hisself, and although it was previously only published twice a year in the past, it will be available four times in 1999. "The Inquirer" transcribes all of the latest Boyds news; including retirements, new releases and upcoming personal appearances, all written in Lowenthal's own unique ("yoonique?") language. Rather than a corporate document, this folksy publication is like getting a letter from a crazy old uncle that you love to hear from. Lowenthal even refers to himself as "Yer Ol' Uncle Bean," strengthening that feeling of family that surrounds the world of Boyds.

WE ARE FAMILY!

Among other things, Lowenthal is first and foremost a family man. Several plush, as well as resin, pieces have been named for his friends and relatives, and even the family dog! The Head Bean admits that the limited edition pieces "Bailey" and "Matthew" are "very special" to him, as they are named after his children, Bailey Anne and Matthew Harrison. Family is a recurrent theme in the Boyds line, as aunts, uncles, cousins and grandparents are all scattered throughout the collection, each connected in one way or another.

Gary is just as adored by his family of Boyds fans and followers as he is by his family at home. Over the years, his popularity has won him a kind of "rock star" status within the world of collectibles. His appearances at collector shows often require crowd control and, in one instance, caused a "Boyds Retail Inquirer" headline to proclaim, only half-jokingly, "The Head Bean Survives Collectors' Expo With All Body Parts Intact!" Another increasingly popular venue for a Gary "sighting" is on the home shopping network, QVC. This season celebrates his fifth year on his own Boyds show as co-host with Senior Program Host Mary Beth Roe.

BLOWING THEM OUT OF THE WATER

Before his success as a collectibles artist, Gary owned an antique shop in rural Maryland where he sold his own line of hand-carved duck decoys. Always the perfectionist, Gary once told QVC viewers that he tried to give his decoys a "used" look by shooting them full of holes. Unfortunately, he only succeeded in blowing them apart.

MINDS THEY ARE A-CHANGING!

It may be the perfectionist in Gary Lowenthal that makes The Boyds Collection Ltd. so successful. Gary will not settle for something that he feels is inferior and he has been known to change design details at the last minute. For example, "Corinna," a 16" plush bear and 1996 TOBY Public's Choice Award winner, seems to have pawed her way into the hair dye on more than one occasion. She has been seen sporting golden tan fur as well as a dark brown coat.

Another incident where Lowenthal made late changes to a piece, occurred when he was designing the Spring 1996 Limited Edition, "Bailey." Lowenthal decided at the last minute that he preferred a dusty rose color for Bailey's dress rather than the original purple that had been chosen. By this time, 3,600 pieces had already been produced and shipped to QVC, since the network purchases product much in advance. Since it was too late to have the new "Bailey" shipped, QVC sold the purple-attired version, who quickly became known as "Hooker Bailey" by Boyds Collection employees, who claimed that the shiny purple material looked less than pristine. The dark purple variation has since become very valuable on the secondary market.

Lowenthal's demand for perfection, combined with his talent for incorporating fun and whimsy into his line of plush animals, is a winning formula that will ensure success for years to come. As collector Kelly Brannon of Arizona says, "It's like they say, never make eye contact with a bear, or you know it will be going home with you. There is definitely something very unique about the Boyds collection. It keeps us going back for more and more."

*W*hile many people say that nothing in life follows a straight line, anyone familiar with the often crooked path of The Boyds Collection Ltd. and its zany creator, Gary Lowenthal, can truly attest to that. With the spirit of ingenuity, a little creativity and perhaps a little luck, the Boyds collection has grown to become one of the most successful product lines in the history of collectibles. It was not always that way, however, as Gary's early years in business were more or less a series of starts and stops.

BIG CITY LIFE

After growing up in Manhattan, Gary Lowenthal headed for college in upstate New York. In just five short years he graduated from Alfred University with both a bachelor's and master's degree in biology. Eager to see the world, he headed for the Fiji Islands with the U.S. Peace Corps where he taught everything from science to sports. Once his time with the Peace Corps had come to a close, Gary again packed his bags, this time content with the idea of a return trip home. He headed back to New York City where he proceeded to spend the next seven years as a purchasing, design and merchandising representative for Bloomingdales.

ONCE UPON A TIME IN A LITTLE TOWN NAMED BOYDS

Although Gary was involved in various creative positions at Bloomingdales (including suitor to fellow employee and future wife, Tina), he soon realized that the corporate world was not for him. Gary longed for a more carefree way of life than the fast-paced city provided, so he packed up his things (and Tina) and headed for the small town of Boyds, Maryland. It was not all fun in the sun, however, and Gary and Tina soon realized they needed to make a living. So, to suit their creative sides, the now Mr. and Mrs. Lowenthal opened a shop called The Boyds Collection Ltd. and started selling antiques.

The antiques business got old quickly, however, so the Lowenthals looked elsewhere for their next business idea. Ever the innovators, the couple turned from antiquities and decided to spend some time in the great outdoors, planting and drying flowers. The flowers would be used for decorative wreaths that Gary and Tina would design, create and sell to stores. Unfortunately, it turned out to be a slow-growing business, so again they moved on.

The next venture (or perhaps, adventure) would turn the Lowenthals into basket cases, so to speak. After the flower business dried up, Tina (whose full name is Justina) began producing handmade oak baskets, that they would then try to wholesale as well. As Gary would later say ". . . Longaberger we weren't!" So, again, the Lowenthals began their search anew for a no-fail business plan.

SEND IN THE DECOYS!

Their next idea would be their first to show signs of the tremendous success that would follow. A few years after their move to Maryland, the Head Bean, as Gary is affectionately known, came up with the idea of creating a line of wooden duck decoys. All the decoys were hand-painted by Gary, and, in the true spirit of a "mom-and-pop" organization, were sealed with wax and then shipped by Tina (rumor is that they were even shot full of holes by Gary, to give them a used look). The business was fast-paced, with Gary and Tina usually completing about 30 on any given day. Finally, the business was a success, albeit not on the level of what they've built today. The decoys were popular, but they hardly flew off the shelves!

C.E.O. Goes Corporate

In April 1998, the investment firm of Kohlberg, Kravis and Roberts (KKR) acquired The Boyds Collection Ltd. Retailers and collectors alike wondered what would happen to the collection and the owner that they fell in love with when the "corporate world" stepped in. However, Lowenthal stepped up to assure everyone that all would be well and in fact, he just needed help in running such a large company. This agreement would actually allow the artist to step away from all the technicalities and politics of the business world and focus on what it is that he really enjoys: cultivating his creative genius.

Banking on the success of the decoys, the Lowenthals again looked to branch out their growing business. So, in their first attempt at a collectible line, Gary and Tina created "Gnomes Homes." The Gnomes Homes where tiny cottages that were made from ceramic and, again, all the work was done by Gary and Tina, alone; including the hand-painting, packaging and distribution. It wouldn't be long, however, before the husband and wife team would find that the company would outgrow even their wildest dreams.

Bearly Able To Be Contained!

Gary and Tina's dedication was about to pay off in a big way. Always the entrepreneur, Gary began to look for even more ways to expand the Boyds business. So, in the early-1980s, Gary began (along with designer Gae Sharp) to design the first of nearly 1,000 bears, hares, cows, cats and other assorted animals that would prove that even grown-ups can't resist the charms of a well-made plush companion.

In 1987, the Lowenthals and their growing company moved to Gettysburg, Pennsylvania. Once the plush line had taken off, Gary, not one to sit around on his well-deserved laurels, proceeded to create new and inventive products. In 1991, Gary proudly "gave birth" to a new baby, better known as the resin figurines. Today the resin lines have grown at a phenomenal rate; currently including five separate lines.

Hand in hand with the advent of Gary's playful, plush empire has come a collector following the likes of which has never been seen in the industry before. At shows, "The Head Bean Chat," as his seminars are known, have become one of the hottest tickets in town! Signing appearances always involve long lines, mostly due in part to his desire to listen to what collectors have to say, no matter if it causes a few delays.

A BEARY HAPPY ANNIVERSARY!

Although those who have been involved with the Boyds line since the beginning would hardly believe it, 1999 has brought about a monumental event in Boyds history: their 20th anniversary! Following on the heels of the five year celebration of the resin line, this newest milestone is sure to be one that collectors won't soon forget! Sure enough, Gary has not forgotten. In a recent edition of *The Boyds Bear Retail Inquirer*, the Head Bean took some time out of his busy schedule to thank all those who, as he put it "Brung Him to the Dance!!" So, while The Boyds Collection Ltd. has grown, and will continue to do so, the spirit behind this enterprising and unique company has hardly been forgotten.

AND THE AWARD GOES TO...

The Boyds Collection Ltd.'s commitment to producing an outstanding product has truly paid off. In 1998, Boyds. won The Collectors' Choice Award for "Best Manufactured Teddy Bears" as well as several achievement awards from the National Association of Limited Edition Dealers (NALED). And The Head Bean Hisself earned the honor of becoming the "Central Pennsylvania Entrepreneur of the Year." This comes on the heels of his 1997 "Artist of the Year" NALED award. In addition, Boyds pieces have won several Golden Teddy and TOBY awards. Both "Corinna" and "Noah & Co . . . Ark Builders" were honored with the 1996 TOBY Public's Choice Award from *Teddy Bear And Friends* magazine, while "Neville . . . Compubear" followed suit in 1997.

Interview With Mary Beth Roe

*C*heckerBee Publishing recently asked QVC Senior Program Host Mary Beth Roe to share some of her thoughts about Boyds Bears and Gary Lowenthal. Here's what she had to say:

CheckerBee: When you received your B.A. in Speech And Communications, I bet you had absolutely no idea that someday you'd be matching wits with a character like Gary Lowenthal. How did you get the honor of being the host of this show?

Mary Beth: Actually, the way that I became the host of the show was really probably more happenstance than anything. At the time, I was the host doing most of the bear shows. I starting selling bears on QVC with Annette Funicello's collectible teddy bear line. And that happened before Boyds Bears came to QVC. I was selling a lot of the bears and I think when Boyds Bears came to QVC, they just thought it would be kind of a natural niche for me to do his bears as well. At the time, I had never heard of Boyds Bears. I had seen them in the stores, but never really knew what I was looking at. I had no clue who Gary Lowenthal was or what he was like until we did our first show together. And when I first met him, I'll never forget . . . he was very nervous, and he was very quiet. I thought, oh boy, this is going to be a tough guest, because he isn't going to have much to say. Well, little did I know that when the red light came on, suddenly he would have plenty to say. And we just hit it off from the beginning. I love humor and he just was so humorous. That first show had such a great chemistry between the two of us. His bears sold very well and we knew that was the start of a long career together.

CheckerBee: In the quieter moments at collectibles shows, Gary can be very sedate. He's much different on TV, isn't he?

Mary Beth: In person, he's kind of a quiet guy – more reserved and very businesslike, but very nice. He's never been anything but wonderful to me. But when he gets on the air, it's like a whole other part of his personality comes out that the rest of us don't really see otherwise.

CheckerBee: Gary's antics sometimes border on the outrageous on the show. What's it like working with him?

"If I had to describe Boyds Bear collectors, I would say they are people with big, huge hearts . . . they are just some of the nicest people I've ever met."

Mary Beth: When you start to know someone a little better, you feel more allowed to tease each other. The more Gary and I started to get to know each other, the more the teasing started to escalate. When that began to happen, the e-mail and the mail that I got was from Boyds Bears collectors siding with me. They were saying, "I hope he's not offending you. I hope he's not making you upset." He's never offended me, not once. He and I have such a good rapport. But it was so funny because they're such loving people that they started to feel bad for me because he was teasing me so much. But it was all just in fun and they know that.

CheckerBee: Boyds collectors just love his zaniness, don't they?

Mary Beth: They do love it. They eat it up. I'll tell you why people really love that guy. Not only because he's really funny, but he genuinely cares about his customers. And when he goes to signings, he will sign until every single person has every single thing signed. He really started out as just a "mom-and-pop" organization, just him and his wife. And then they got one employee and all this started, and they had started out really very small. So even though he has a big business now, he still has small business mentality in many ways, like in how he cares about his customers. That's one of the things I really respect about him, too.

CheckerBee: You seem to do a good job keeping up with him, is it hard?

Mary Beth: Well, I've learned how to, you know. Now, we have such a good rapport that I feel like I can tease him back a few times. Gary knows me well enough that he knows not to cross the line. There's this imaginary fine line and he'll kind of get up to the line but he won't cross it. And he knows just how much to say and how much not to say. Because he sometimes takes it right up to the line.

CheckerBee: I know you've had the opportunity to meet Gary's wife, have you met his entire family?

Mary Beth: I have. I've met Tina, Matthew and Bailey and they're all just so, so nice. Tina, his wife, is just a joy. She's as funny as he is. She's bubbly and friendly and just a sweetheart of a lady. And we all tease her that being married to Gary hasn't dampened her spirits at all. And his two children are beautiful. He has a wonderful family.

CheckerBee: Boyds collectors seem to have a lighthearted mind-set that seems different than the mind-set of collectors of other lines. How would you describe Boyds collectors?

Mary Beth: If I had to describe Boyds Bear collectors, I would say they are people with big, huge hearts. They're people who are more romantic, more affectionate people, because they're the ones who, literally, when they see those darling little faces go, "Ohh . . . ." When we've had our live audiences, the funny thing is Gary and I will do an autograph signing after the show, and it will take two and a half hours to do the signing just for 150 people, because we stand and talk to them. We're not just autographing the pieces and then they move on. We're chatting with them. We're laughing, we're having fun. It's like a big, huge family. And they are just some of the nicest people I've ever met.

CheckerBee: So do people come up to you on the street and recognize you from the Boyds show?

Mary Beth: Mostly, people would recognize me as the QVC Senior Program Host if they recognize me on the street. A lot of them will come up and say, "I just love watching you and Gary." It's funny because sometimes they'll say, "Boyds," but more often they'll say, "you and Gary." And it's almost become the "Mary Beth and Gary Show." But even when it's Mary Beth and Gary's show, Boyds Bears are still the number one part of the show. That's one thing about being a host on QVC, even though the guest is funny or he and I have a great rapport, my number one mission on every show is that the product is the number one important item. So even though we play and have fun, I always make sure that the product gets described correctly, that any information we have about the product gets out, and that sort of thing, so that when people actually buy the Boyds Bears and they get them home, they know as much about them as we could possibly have told them.

CheckerBee: We've heard that some of the pieces he's created are named after you. How does that feel?

Mary Beth: The only one I can really think of is the doll that was on Today's Special Value last August [1998] on Collectors' Day. And I'll tell you the story behind that. We were actually at the Toy Fair in New York, last February 1998 and Gary and I were standing in his booth, just talking about the product line [with another QVC representative]. Gary looked at me and said, "Well, here's the lady who really knows dolls. Let's ask her." One thing that I love about his fabrics is that some are more on the denim side or the tea-dyed look. He also has some of his bears and rabbits in these velveteen jumpers. And I said, well, most of his

> "First of all, I love his bears. They are the sweetest, cutest little things you ever did see. And then with his humor matched in, it's just such a fun show."

dolls have been done in the tea-dyed fabrics and the denim fabrics, so I said I'd like to see a doll in one of the velveteen, pastel colors, to go with some of the bears and rabbits that are in those velveteen fabrics. And he said, "Yeah, I've never done that before. Maybe that's a great idea." From there, Gary just took my ideas and ran with them, and that's how the "Elizabeth" doll turned out. And he did ask me what I wanted to name it. He wanted to name it Mary Beth, and I said no. I don't like things that focus the attention on me. I wanted the attention to be on the doll. So we just picked my middle name, which is Elizabeth. Some people know that, some people don't. Elizabeth is also a very common name, and a name that a lot of people have in their families or among their friends. It turned out to be a really special doll.

CheckerBee: We have to ask you about his costumes. Are you aware of what he's going to come out as or is it a surprise for you when he walks through the door?

Mary Beth: They never tell me what his costumes are going to be. The only one I knew about this year was the Santa

Claus costume. I asked one of the buyers, "Is he coming out in a Santa Claus outfit or costume at any point?" and they said yes, on the last show of the miniseries. So I got the idea to get the Mrs. Claus outfit to go with it, because I feel like I

never get to wear a costume, and I kind of wanted to. We made it a surprise. He had no idea I was going to be in that costume. But all the other costumes he appeared in, they never tell me ahead of time. And so it's always virtually a surprise. Sometimes I feel a little nervous.

CheckerBee: So you're sitting on the couch waiting for him to walk through that door, and you have no idea what to expect?

Mary Beth: Exactly. Because they want my initial reaction and that's what they get every time.

CheckerBee: You must find the show much different than some of the other ones that you've done, just because of Gary's personality.

Mary Beth: Well, one of the things that I love about the show is that it is different from a lot of the other shows I do. And I love the variety, because I sell everything from jewelry to fashions to cookware to housewares and then, of course, the bears, dolls and collectible lines. First of all, I love his bears. They are the sweetest, cutest little things you ever did see. And then with his humor matched in, it's just such a fun show. It's really not much work. I feel like I get paid to have fun and he's just always great on the show. But the bottom line is the show wouldn't do well if the product wasn't great. And the product that he brings to QVC is truly great quality, with great prices and faces that every one falls in love with.

*T*he Boyds Collection Ltd. adds 97 adorable new plush items to their regular line in 1999. Among these pieces are 45 bears, 25 hares, eight cats, three cows, one lamb, one gorilla, two mice, one frog, two pigs, three dogs and six ornaments. *Important Note: Some photos of the 1999 releases may feature prototypes. See your Boyds retailer for a closer look at the new releases.*

BEARS

Abercrombie B. Beanster (*J.B. Bean & Associates*) . . . Abercrombie is proud to be one of the first in his series to be made with a new design. Compared to other *J.B. Bean & Associates*, Abercrombie features long arms, short legs and his ears and feet are larger than his predecessors.

Auntie Aleena de Bearvoire (*T.J.'s Best Dressed*) . . . Auntie Aleena, well rested after a winter of hibernation, puts on her favorite hat and heads out to visit her favorite niece.

Bailey (*T.J.'s Best Dressed*) . . . "Bailey" and her friends are spending the spring in Paris and she fits right into the fashion capital of the world in a dusty rose cardigan and a rose-topped beret.

Bethany Thistlebeary (*T.J.'s Best Dressed*) . . . This wide-eyed darling longs to be just like her big sister Skylar. She even dresses just like her, right down to the hair bow!

Bixby Trufflebeary (*Bears In The Attic*) . . . Bixby is cream-colored and feels as soft as can be! Once you've experienced a bearhug from Bixby, you'll never want to let him go!

Bradshaw P. Beansford (*J.B. Bean & Associates*) . . . This ginger-colored sweetie will be your best friend if you let him. He's a great listener and an even better hugger!

Bumbershoot B. Jodibear (*T.J.'s Best Dressed*) ... Bumbershoot knows that he must make it through those April showers to enjoy the May flowers and in his yellow slicker and hat, he's prepared!

Buttercup C. Snicklefritz (*BabyBoyds*) ... Although designed with children in mind, collectors of all ages will fall in love with Buttercup's soft, colorful fur!

Carmella de Bearvoire (*T.J.'s Best Dressed*)...Carmella excitedly waits for her Auntie Aleena who is going to take her for a walk in the park and buy her some honey!

Clover L. Buzzoff (*T.J.'s Best Dressed*) ... This bear's love for honey motivates him to go right to the source. Let's hope he doesn't get stung!

Delanie B. Beansford (*J.B. Bean & Associates*) ... It looks like this long-haired cutie forgot to take off his winter coat!

Dilly McDoodle (*BabyBoyds*) ... Dilly's bright fur, the color of sunshine, is sure to brighten up the spirits of any down in the dumps collector!

Edmund (*T.J.'s Best Dressed*) ... Edmund is ready for the crisp Paris weather in his rose and white striped sweater and green corduroy pants.

Forrest B. Bearsley (*T.J.'s Best Dressed*) ... Forrest is irresistible in green corduroy overalls and a matching bow tie.

Gwendina (*T.J.'s Best Dressed*) ... This yellow and white bear may be small but she makes up for her short stature with lots of love! "Gwendina" is always ready to get (and give) hugs!

Harding G. Bearington (*The Mohair Bears*) ... "The bigger, the better" seems to be the motto of this bear, who has outdone himself with a giant blue bow tie.

Hartley B. Mine (*T.J.'s Best Dressed*) ... Hartley wears his love for you on his sleeve (or rather, chest). And who can resist this charming suitor?

Hemingway K. Grizzman (*T.J.'s Best Dressed*) ... "And the one I caught was this big!" This angler is ready for a big day of fishing (and trading tall tales) with his friends.

Henley Fitzhampton (*T.J.'s Best Dressed*) ... While spending the winter travelling with his sister Yardley, Henley has learned everything it takes to be a true sailor, even how to dress!

Honey P. Snicklefritz (*BabyBoyds*) ... Honey is not only baby's best friend; he's mom's little helper! Each of the Snicklefritz bears plays a lullaby to your baby when squeezed!

Jameson J. Bearsford (*The Archive Series*) ... Whether at work or at play, Jameson is always "dressed to the T" in his classy black bow tie with paw-print accents.

Katie B. Berrijam (*T.J.'s Best Dressed*) ... Katie has been waiting all winter to wear her colorful floral dress and hair bow which perfectly complements her soft white fur!

Laurel S. Berrijam (*T.J.'s Best Dressed*) ... The smallest of the Berrijam sisters, Laurel shows off her new romper before heading out to play.

Lincoln B. Bearington (*The Mohair Bears*) ... This stately honey-colored bear looks regal in a purple bow tie.

Liza J. Berrijam (*T.J.'s Best Dressed*) ... Liza knows that springtime means lots of work as well as fun, so she's dressed in a floral jumper for easy movement and a matching hairband to keep her fur out of her eyes.

Marlowe Snoopstein (*T.J.'s Best Dressed*) ... This "hare" has found a sneaky way to get his favorite food.

Minnie Higgenthorpe (*T.J.'s Best Dressed*) ... In celebration of springtime, Minnie wears the biggest flower she could find. Not only does she look stunning, but she smells good too!

Mrs. Mertz (*T.J.'s Best Dressed*) ... Mrs. Mertz looks as though she just returned from the beauty parlor and is all ready for an afternoon of tea and gossip with the ladies!

Oxford T. Bearrister (*The Archive Series*) ... This tan bear with a spiffy ribbon hopes he looks good enough to catch your eye so you'll take him home with you!

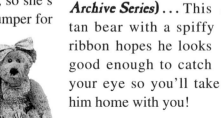

Perriwinkle P. Snicklefritz (*BabyBoyds*) ... There's no question where this bear got his unique name – it looks like he's been playing in the fur dye!

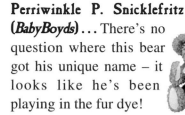

Prudence Bearimore (*T.J.'s Best Dressed*) ... A true romantic, Prudence celebrates Valentine's Day all year round! To help keep her inspired, she wears a red and white plaid dress adorned with hearts.

Quincy B. Bibbly (*T.J.'s Best Dressed*) ... Quincy realizes that his long paws make it difficult to eat with, so he's come prepared! His denim bib, customized with the Boyds Bears logo, might not stay clean, but he will!

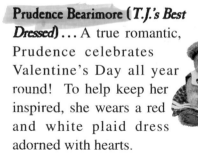

Skylar Thistlebeary (*T.J.'s Best Dressed*)... Skylar anxiously awaits the warm days of spring and skies that are as blue as her dress!

Stevenson Q. Bearitage (*T.J.'s Best Dressed*)... This patriotic teddy is decked out in his red, white and blue sweater in anticipation of fireworks and 4th of July picnics.

Tatum F. Wuzzie (*T.F. Wuzzies*)... Although Tatum is small, she makes a big impression in this adorable sundress and matching hat!

Thisbey F. Wuzzie (*T.F. Wuzzies*)... One of the three patriotic red, white and blue *Wuzzies*, Twilight blushes at the thought of getting to spend his favorite holiday, Independence Day, in your home.

Tilly F. Wuzzie (*T.F. Wuzzies*)... Tilly just can't wait for Easter this year! So he waits patiently in his disguise, hoping he'll get picked to be the Easter Bunny's helper!

Tootie F. Wuzzie (*T.F. Wuzzies*)... Tootie and her friends Thisbey and Twilight ring in the new year the All-American way!

Townsend Q. Bearrister (*The Archive Series*)... A darker version of his brother Oxford, Townsend comes wearing nothing but a spiffy bow.

Twilight F. Wuzzie (*T.F. Wuzzies*)... This bear is feeling a little blue! Cheer her up by bringing her home to join the rest of your Boyds buddies!

Wilcox J. Beansford (*J.B. Bean & Associates*)... You can always count on Wilcox, a classic brown teddy, for a hug just when you need one most!

WHAT'S NEW FOR BOYDS PLUSH ANIMALS

Winnie Wuzzwhite (*T.J.'s Best Dressed*) . . . Winnie was white? She still is white, at least until the weather gets nice and she can play outside!

Woodrow T. Bearington (*The Mohair Bears*) . . . A member of the new soft-body *Mohairs*, Woodrow may look stiff, but he is a great cuddler!

Yardley Fitzhampton (*T.J.'s Best Dressed*) . . . Straight off the U.S.S. Boyds comes Miss Yardley, the world traveller, who has bundles of interesting stories to tell.

Yvette DuBeary (*T.J.'s Best Dressed*) . . . It's time to get out of the house to go visit friends and no one knows that better than Yvette, who threw on a brightly colored hat before heading out the door.

CATS

Boots Alleyruckus (*J.B. Bean & Associates*) . . . Despite the superstition, you'll want this adorable black cat to cross your path!

Claudine de la Plumtete (*T.J.'s Best Dressed*) . . . This off-white feline has taken the adage "a feather in your cap" quite literally and is all set to be the newest tabby trendsetter!

Kattelina Purrsley (*T.J.'s Best Dressed*) . . . Kattelina looks absolutely "purrfect" in her violet jumper and matching ear bow.

Kitt Purrsley (*T.J.'s Best Dressed*) . . . Although Kitt's thick white fur protects him from the last of the winter chills, he can't bear to part with his favorite sweater.

Lindbergh Cattington (*The Mohair Bears*) . . . Cat lovers will never have to worry about this friendly feline scratching up their furniture.

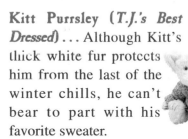

COLLECTOR'S
VALUE GUIDE™

Lola Ninelives (*T.J.'s Best Dressed*) ... Cat lovers everywhere will be smitten with this feline femme fatale. Lola's soft white fur is perfectly groomed and decorated by a green neck-ribbon and a rose-topped hat.

Tabby F. Wuzzie (*T.F. Wuzzies*) ... The first cat to join the *Wuzzies*, Tabby is smaller than most mice!

Zachariah Alleyruckus (*J.B. Bean & Associates*) ... This brownish-gray tabby is constantly getting into trouble, but always manages to land on his feet!

COWS

Angus MacMoo (*T.J.'s Best Dressed*) ... This well-dressed heifer looks "udderly" marvelous in his overalls and red plaid ribbon. And as well dressed as he is, he's ready for the honor of being the first cow to stampede into the *T.J.'s Best Dressed* series.

Ernestine Vanderhoof (*Animal Menagerie*) ... A new addition to the Boyds bovine collection, this chocolate and white cow wants to be part of your herd.

Silo Q. Vanderhoof (*Animal Menagerie*) ... Cow lovers will find Silo, who's dressed in a red bow, "moost" endearing.

DOGS

Barkley McFarkle (*BabyBoyds*) ... This lovable little pooch is the perfect companion for your baby; he's extra soft and extra huggable.

Philo Puddlemaker (*Bears In The Attic*) ... This Boston Terrier promises he won't live up to his name if you take him home with you!

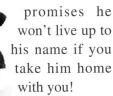

Toby F. Wuzzie (*T.F. Wuzzies*)... Toby's bark is the biggest thing about him! This pint-sized pooch is the first of his kind to join the *T.F. Wuzzies* series.

FROGS

G. Kelly Ribbit (*T.J.'s Best Dressed*) ... As the storm begins, the skies are filled with the sounds of raindrops hitting the pavement, lightning crashing and . . . frogs singing? Decked out in a slicker and matching hat, this harmonious croaker plays "Singin' In The Rain."

GORILLAS

Viola Magillacuddy (*T.J.'s Best Dressed*) ... Viola looks "apesolutely" fabulous in her Sunday best. She is dressed in a straw hat (to keep the sun out of her eyes), a bright purple bow and a matching flower.

HARES

Dudley Hopson (*T.J.'s Best Dressed*) ... This cotton-tailed cutie looks absolutely adorable in his blue jumpsuit and bow tie.

Earhart Harington (*The Mohair Bears*) ... With short mohair fur and a face that cries out to be loved, this adorable orphan is sure to disappear from shelves as a popular addition to the mini "mo-hares."

Edith Q. Harington (*The Mohair Bears*) ... Edith is the latest hare to join the ranks of the *Mohairs* and her fur is still a little ruffled from all the "hare-raising" excitement!

Emily Babbit (*T.J.'s Best Dressed*) ... Wearing an adorable embroidered apron and a rose behind her ear, Emily looks as though she's begun feeling spring fever a bit early!

Fern Blumenshine (*T.J.'s Best Dressed***)** ... Fern can't contain her excitement for the upcoming season! She hopes to meet her idol, the Easter Bunny!

Flossie B. Hopplebuns (*Bears In The Attic***)** ... This fluffy bunny makes a great bedtime companion! Her cream-colored fur and squeezable body make her the perfect p.m. pet!

Greta de la Fleur (*T.J.'s Best Dressed***)** ... Although she still has a little growing to do before it fits her, Greta insists on wearing her pink flowered hat in the spirit of the spring season.

Harvey P. Hoppleby (*BabyBoyds***)** ... While he's extra gentle with your baby, Harvey was made extra tough inside, so he can withstand the tugs and tumbles of young ones!

Iris Rosenbunny (*T.J.'s Best Dressed***)** ... This blue-eyed beauty, dressed in her very best lavender jumper and bow, hopes to become a part of your family.

Juliana Hopkins (*T.J.'s Best Dressed***)** ... Juliana is dressed for a fine spring day with her raspberry jumper and hair bow.

Kerry Q. Hopgood (*J.B. Bean & Associates***)** ... This long eared bunny's favorite hoppy (er . . . hobby) is to kick back and relax after a long day.

Lady Harriwell (*T.J.'s Best Dressed***)** ... This lovely lady is not afraid to let her true colors shine! She is so excited about the upcoming season that even her fur is beginning to celebrate!

Libby Lapinette (*T.J.'s Best Dressed***)** ... Little Libby, anxious to experience her first springtime, eagerly awaits the warmer weather in her yellow jumper.

Lucinda de la Fleur (*T.J.'s Best Dressed*) . . . Lucinda, an extremely shy hare, peers out from underneath a pastel pink hat to get a look at the world.

Marigold McHare (*J.B. Bean & Associates*) . . . Not only is Marigold's fur made of gold, but her heart is too! She is as beautiful on the inside as she is on the outside!

Millie Hopkins (*T.J.'s Best Dressed*)...Millie has found a clever way to keep the freshly bloomed flowers with her all through the year; she has sewn them onto a cozy rose sweater!

Miranda Blumenshine (*T.J.'s Best Dressed*) . . . Miranda's floral dress is the color of her favorite food, lettuce leaves!

Pansy Rosenbunny (*T.J.'s Best Dressed*)... With wide-eyed wonder, Pansy watches the snow melt and the trees begin to blossom as the warmer weather rolls around.

Rosalynn P. Harington (*The Mohair Bears*) . . . While she looks cool and collected on the outside, Rosalynn is really a big softie on the inside! She is one of the new, softer *Mohairs*, made to be squeezed!

Roscoe P. Bumpercrop (*T.J.'s Best Dressed*)... Roscoe is one of the taller bunnies in the Boyds line, so he needs extra food to keep up his strength. He always remembers to bring along a carrot for those emergency snack attacks!

Taffy C. Hopplebuns (*Bears In The Attic*) . . . This bunny is sure to be as sweet as the candy she was named for and from the looks of her paws, she's been playing in the powdered sugar!

Tami F. Wuzzie (*T.F. Wuzzies*)... Tami puts on her gardening gear before heading out to the garden for a day of planting her favorite food, carrots!

Tapper F. Wuzzie (*T.F. Wuzzies*)... This gray and white hare is the perfect addition for any Boyds collector's Easter basket!

Vanessa D. LaPinne (*T.J.'s Best Dressed*)... Vanessa dresses only in the best and always puts on a winning smile! Will she be able to win your heart?

Wedgewood J. Hopgood (*J.B. Bean & Associates*)... Wedgewood, a stunning white hare, is named for the colorful pads on his ears and paws. He adds a matching blue ribbon to accentuate the look.

LAMBS

Wannabee Ewe-Too (*T.J.'s Best Dressed*)... The only lamb debuting in this season's lineup, Wannabee is adorable in a raspberry sweater and a big smile!

MICE

Cottage McNibble (*T.J.'s Best Dressed*)... Hide the cats and stock up on cheese, because you'll want to take Cottage home the minute you lay eyes on her! She's irresistible in her denim jumper and red hair bow!

Sharp McNibble (*T.J.'s Best Dressed*)... In their denim overalls, Sharp and his sister Cottage fit right into the laid-back way of farm life.

PIGS

Kaitlin K. Trufflesnout (*T.J.'s Best Dressed*)... This cutie "hams it up" in her new green outfit.

Primrose P. Trufflesnout (*T.J.'s Best Dressed*) . . . Primrose won't be doing any rolling in the mud today! She looks magnificent in her green floral print dress.

ORNAMENTS

Aurora Goodnight . . . Aurora, one of the guardian angels of the Boyds collection, watches over her friends and protects them from harm!

Bibi Buzzby . . . Bibi is sure to buzz right into your heart once you set eyes on her. She is the sweetest bee you'll ever see!

Bud Buzzby . . . This handsome "honey" liked his Halloween costume so much, he refuses to take it off!

Echo Goodnight . . . This purple and white angel bear has been given wings so she can bring her warmth and love right to you!

Moondust Goodspeed . . . Although he's arrived a little early for Christmas, this ornament makes a great accessory anywhere around the house!

Stardust Goodspeed . . . This bunny's outfit is decorated with flowers, making her the sweetest smelling angel under the heavens!

Collector's Club

*T*he Loyal Order of Friends of Boyds, that "Slightly Off-Center Collector's Club for people who still believe in . . . Bears And Hares You Can Trust™," will celebrate its third birthday in 1999. And, popular since its inception, this club is is showing no signs of slowing down!

The club was started in June 1996 and to say it was a success would be an understatement. The demand for membership in the first year was so overwhelming that The Boyds Collection Ltd. could barely keep up with orders and, in fact, many members did not receive their charter kits until much later in the year. Since then, the club has continued to grow and, today, it boasts well over 100,000 members (a.k.a. F.o.B.s or "Friends of Boyds").

The 1999 F.o.B. application is, in part, the tale of Flora Mae Berriweather and her daughter Blossum. Blossum, eager to be a gardening success like her Mom, learns the three secrets to gardening (and life) as she cultivates her sunflower to be a prize winner.

The three secrets imparted by Flora Mae, "Plant with Hope . . . Grow with Love . . . Bloom with Joy!" are incorporated into all of this year's club pieces. Boyds collectors who join or renew their membership in 1999 will receive two exclusive pieces to remind them of this adage well past gardening season. "Flora Mae Berriweather" is an adorable 6" plush piece, dressed in a handknit sweater and a matching sunflower-adorned hat and "Blossum B. Berriweather . . . Bloom With Joy!" is an exclusive resin figurine featuring Blossum under her award-winning sunflower which measures over 4" tall.

In addition, club members will receive a genuine "Bloomin' F.o.B. Sunflower Seed Packet" so that, when the time is right, they can start their own prize-winning garden.

Also included in membership is a year's subscription to the "F.o.B. Inquirer," the official Boyds newsletter written by the "Head Bean Hisself." And, for the first time, the "Inquirer" will be published four times a year, instead of just two!

Like in years past, along with this year's other club specials, members will also receive a national directory of Boyds dealers, a color catalog, a Boyds product list and an "Bloomin' F.o.B." pin.

Members will also be offered the opportunity to purchase other club exclusive pieces (as well as an F.o.B. mug) by sending in the Redemption Certificates that are included in the membership kit. "Plant With Hope, Grow With Love, Bloom With Joy" is a set of three "Members Only" plush bears created with this year's theme in mind, while "Sunny And Sally Berriweather . . . Plant With Hope" is the 1999 Bearstone piece. And the club helps celebrate the introduction of the new *Noah's Pageant Series* with it's own addition, "Noah's Genius At Work Table."

Club membership cost for one year is $32.50 (while the club is blooming, the price is not) and members must have their applications in by December 31, 1999 to take advantage of club benefits. A "Bloomin' F.o.B." membership application can be found at the back of this book or at your local Boyds retailer. Applications should be sent to:

The Loyal Order of Friends of Boyds
The Boyds Collection Ltd.
P. O. Box 4386, F.o.B. Dept.
Gettysburg, PA 17325-4386

FUTURE RETIREMENTS

Retirements

*T*he Boyds Collection Ltd. uses two methods to retire pieces: a "scheduled retirement," which is a retirement announced in advance, allowing retailers to continue to order these pieces until almost the end of the year; or a "sudden death retirement," which means that once the stock of that particular piece in the warehouse is exhausted, the piece is gone. The following is a list of pieces scheduled to be retired during 1999, with issue year, item number and series abbreviation in parentheses (*see chart on page 46*).

RETIRING IN 1999!

BEARS

- ❏ Alouetta de Grizetta (1996, #91842, TJ)
- ❏ Bailey (Spring 1998, #9199-09, TJ)
- ❏ Bailey (Fall 1998, #9199-10, TJ)
- ❏ Barnaby B. Bean (1994, #5150-03, JB)
- ❏ Baxter B. Bean (1994, #5151-05, JB)
- ❏ Becky (1996, #91395-01, TJ)
- ❏ Bosley (1997, #91561, TJ)
- ❏ Delmarva V. Crackenpot (1997, #91002, TJ)
- ❏ Edmund (Spring 1998, #9175-09, TJ)
- ❏ Edmund (Fall 1998, #9175-10, TJ)
- ❏ Emmett Elfberg (1996, #917305, TJ)
- ❏ Emmy Lou (1996, #91001, TJ)
- ❏ Ethan (1998, #917322, TJ)
- ❏ Harding G. Bearington (1999, #590051-01, MB)
- ❏ Leon (1993, #1001-08, CC)

- ❏ Lincoln B. Bearington (1999, #590022-08, MB)
- ❏ Matthew (Fall 1998, #91756-10, TJ)
- ❏ Matthew H. Growler (1996, #5721, AS)
- ❏ Perceval (1992, #5703-08, AS)
- ❏ Slugger (1996, #9177-01, TJ)
- ❏ Watson (1993, #9187, TJ)
- ❏ Woodrow T. Bearington
    (1999, #590041-03, MB)

CATS

- ❏ Browning (1992, #5741, AS)
- ❏ Byron (1992, #5740, AS)
- ❏ Opel Catberg (1995, #5324-10, JB)
- ❏ Thoreau (1995, #5740-08, AS)
- ❏ Zoe R. Grimilkin (1994, #5304-07, JB)

DOGS

- ❏ Indy (Fall 1998, 91757-10, TJ)

FROGS

- ❏ Jeremiah B. Ribbit (1997, #566450, BA)

HARES

- ❏ Daffodil de la Hoppsack (1998, #91404, BY)
- ❏ Edith Q. Harington (1999, #590160-03, MB)
- ❏ Emily Babbit (Spring 1998, #9150-09, TJ)
- ❏ Emily Babbit (Fall 1998, #9150-10, TJ)
- ❏ Gretchen (1998, #911210, TJ)
- ❏ Hannah (1997, #91111, TJ)
- ❏ Hopkins (1998, #91121, TJ)
- ❏ Lady Pembrooke
    (1997, #91892-09, TJ)
- ❏ Orchid de la Hoppsack
    (1998, #91405, BY)
- ❏ Rosalynn P. Harington
    (1999, #590140-01, MB)

PIGS

- ❏ Kaitlin McSwine
    (1997, #91601, TJ)

ORNAMENTS

- ❏ Gweneth (1997, #56031)
- ❏ Celeste (1994, #5609-01)
- ❏ Immanuella (1996, #5609-09)

*T*his section showcases the ten most valuable Boyds plush animals as determined by their values on the secondary market. In order to qualify for this section, the piece must have top dollar value and show an increase in value from its original price. Secondary market values for some older Boyds plush animals have not been established. As a result, several rare and valuable pieces do not appear on this list but are extremely coveted by collectors! (Please note, this list does not include Boyds plush exclusives.)

Bailey (Fall 1992)
Issued 1992 – Retired 1993
Original Price: N/A
Secondary Market Value: **$700**

Rudolf
Issued 1992 – Retired 1992
Original Price: N/A
Secondary Market Value: **$580**

PHOTO
UNAVAILABLE

Eleanor Bear (set/3)
Issued 1990 – Retired 1990
Original Price: N/A
Secondary Market Value: **$575**

Beatrice
Issued 1991 – Retired 1991
Original Price: $63
Secondary Market Value: **$435**

Nana
Issued 1991 – Retired 1992
Original Price: $27
Secondary Market Value: **$420**

Memsy
Issued N/A – Retired N/A
Original Price: N/A
Secondary Market Value: **$385**

Mrs. Bearberry
Issued N/A – Retired N/A
Original Price: N/A
Secondary Market Value: **$375**

Bailey (Spring 1993)
Issued 1993 – Retired 1994
Original Price: N/A
Secondary Market Value: **$350**

Phillip Bear Hop
Issued 1991 – Retired 1992
Original Price: $27
Secondary Market Value: **$330**

Kris Moose
Issued 1992 – Retired 1996
Original Price: $27
Secondary Market Value: **$320**

HOW TO USE YOUR VALUE GUIDE

Adams F. Bearington
6" • #590080-03 • MB
Issued: 1998 • Retired: 1998
Orig. Price: $18 • **Value: $37**

1. LOCATE your piece in the Value Guide. Each piece appears alphabetically within its animal type, with the categories listed in the following order: *bears, cats, cows, crows, dogs, donkeys, elephants, frogs, gorillas, hares, lambs, lions, mice, monkeys, moose, pigs, ornaments and collector's club pieces.* Exclusive pieces follow the ornaments and are also in alphabetical order within each animal type. You can also use the handy *Bearfinder – Alphabetical Index*, beginning on page 211 to help you quickly find your piece. A guide to the abbreviations of the plush series appears below.

2. RECORD both the original price that you paid and the current value of the piece in the corresponding boxes at the bottom of the page. Pieces for which a secondary market price has not been established are listed as "N/E." For those, write the price you paid in the "Value Of My Collection" column. The market value for current pieces is the 1999 suggested retail price (although retail prices may vary).

3. CALCULATE the value for each page by adding together all of the boxes in each column and recording it in the "Pencil Totals" section at the bottom of the box. Be sure to use a pencil so you can change the totals as your Boyds plush collection grows!

4. TRANSFER the totals from each page to the "Total Value Of My Collection" worksheets located at the end of the Value Guide section.

5. ADD the totals together to determine the overall value of your collection.

BEARS	
Price Paid	Value Of My Collection
1.	
2.	
3.	**18** ─ **37**
4.	
5.	
PENCIL TOTALS	

PLUSH SERIES KEY

AR The Artisan Series	**CC** Clintons Cabinet	**HT** Hares in Toyland	**SB** Snow Bears
AS The Archive Series	**CH** The Choir Hares	**JB** J.B. Bean & Associates	**SQ** Squeekies
BA Bears In The Attic	**DB** Doodle Bears	**MB** The Mohair Bears	**TF** T.F.Wuzzies
BB The Bubba Bears	**FL** The Flatties	**NL** Northern Lights	**TJ** T.J.'s Best Dressed
BY BabyBoyds	**GB** Grizzly Bears	**OR** Ornaments	**WB** Wool Boyds Series
CB The Choir Bears	**HD** Himalayan Dancing Bears	**PM** Prime Minister's Cabinet	

BOYDS PLUSH ANIMALS

No matter what kind of animal you prefer, you are sure to find one (or hundreds) to fit your style within the Boyds plush line. From a traditional brown antique-looking teddy bear to a bean-filled, purple hare, the Boyds collection includes over 1,000 characters, each of which is unique in its very own way.

BEARS

Bears continue to be the largest and most popular category of Boyds plush line, with well over 150 of these cute and cuddly creatures currently available. In 1999, 45 new bears will take center stage, while 22 will head into hibernation by the time the year comes to a close.

① New!

Abercrombie B. Beanster
16" • #510400-05 • JB
Issued: 1999 • Current
Orig. Price: $26 • **Value: $26**

②

Ace Bruin
10" • #5122 • JB
Issued: Pre-1990 • Retired: 1996
Orig. Price: $14 • **Value: $40**

③

Adams F. Bearington
6" • #590080-03 • MB
Issued: 1998 • Retired: 1998
Orig. Price: $18 • **Value: $37**

④

Addington
12" • #5701-05 • AS
Issued: 1993 • Retired: 1996
Orig. Price: $20 • **Value: $45**

⑤

Alastair
5.5" • #5725-08 • AS
Issued: 1996 • Retired: 1997
Orig. Price: $7 • **Value: $19**

BEARS

	Price Paid	Value Of My Collection
1.		
2.		
3.		
4.		
5.		

✎ PENCIL TOTALS

①

Alastair & Camilla
(set/2, bear and hare)
N/A • #98042 • TJ
Issued: 1996 • Retired: 1996
Orig. Price: N/A • **Value: $42**

②

Albert B. Bean
14" • #5123-03 • JB
Issued: 1993 • Retired: 1997
Orig. Price: $20 • **Value: $32**

③

Alec
(also known as "Alex")
5.5" • #5711 • AS
Issued: 1990 • Retired: 1991
Orig. Price: $7 • **Value: $82**

④

Aletha...
The Bearmaker (LE-500)
N/A • #9217 • N/A
Issued: 1994 • Retired: 1994
Orig. Price: $74 • **Value: $260**

⑤

Alexis Berriman
16" • #912022 • TJ
Issued: 1998 • Current
Orig. Price: $61 • **Value: $61**

⑥

Alice
11" • #1101-08 • CC
Issued: 1995 • Retired: 1995
Orig. Price: $12 • **Value: $22**

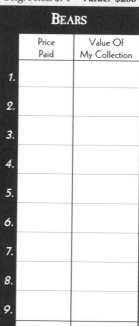

BEARS

	Price Paid	Value Of My Collection
1.		
2.		
3.		
4.		
5.		
6.		
7.		
8.		
9.		

✎ PENCIL TOTALS

⑦

Alice II
11" • #1101-08 • CC
Issued: 1996 • Retired: 1998
Orig. Price: $12 • **Value: $18**

⑧

Alouetta de Grizetta
6" • #91842 • TJ
Issued: 1996 • To Be Retired: 1999
Orig. Price: $9 • **Value: $9**

⑨

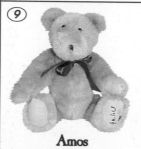

Amos
12" • #5700-03 • AS
Issued: 1995 • Retired: 1995
Orig. Price: $20 • **Value: $175**

①

Andrei Berriman
5.5" • #917300-06 • TJ
Issued: 1998 • Current
Orig. Price: $13 • **Value: $13**

②

Ansel
6" • #91271 • TJ
Issued: 1996 • Current
Orig. Price: $13 • **Value: $13**

③

Archibald McBearlie
6" • #91393 • TJ
Issued: 1998 • Current
Orig. Price: $13 • **Value: $13**

④
PHOTO UNAVAILABLE

Arctic Bear
info unavailable
Orig. Price: N/A • **Value: N/E**

⑤

Arlo
8" • #9141 • TJ
Issued: 1994 • Retired: 1996
Orig. Price: $12 • **Value: $45**

⑥

Arlo
8 • #98040 • TJ
Issued: 1996 • Retired: 1997
Orig. Price: $12 • **Value: $40**

⑦

Artemus
8" • #1003-08 • CC
Issued: 1997 • Current
Orig. Price: $7 • **Value: $7**

⑧

Arthur
16" • #5712 • AS
Issued: 1991 • Retired: 1992
Orig. Price: $32 • **Value: $140**

⑨

Ashley
14" • #5109 • JB
Issued: 1991 • Retired: 1992
Orig. Price: $20 • **Value: N/E**

⑩

Asquith
8" • #5705-05 • AS
Issued: 1993 • Retired: 1995
Orig. Price: $13 • **Value: $37**

BEARS

	Price Paid	Value Of My Collection
1.		
2.		
3.		
4.		
5.		
6.		
7.		
8.		
9.		
10.		

PENCIL TOTALS

①

Astrid
9" • #9137 • TJ
Issued: 1994 • Retired: 1996
Orig. Price: $20 • **Value: $43**

②

Attlee
8" • #5705B • AS
Issued: 1992 • Retired: 1993
Orig. Price: N/A • **Value: $92**

③

Auggie Bruin
16" • #5125 • JB
Issued: 1992 • Retired: 1996
Orig. Price: $27 • **Value: $60**

④

Augusta
14" • #91010 • TJ
Issued: 1998 • Retired: 1998
Orig. Price: $36 • **Value: $44**

⑤

Aunt Becky Bearchild
12" • #912052 • TJ
Issued: 1998 • Current
Orig. Price: $29 • **Value: $29**

⑥

Aunt Bessie Skidoo
9" • #91931 • TJ
Issued: 1998 • Current
Orig. Price: $30 • **Value: $30**

⑦

Aunt Yvonne Dubeary
11" • #918450 • TJ
Issued: 1998 • Current
Orig. Price: $25 • **Value: $25**

⑧

New!

Auntie Aleena de Bearvoire
10" • #918451 • TJ
Issued: 1999 • Current
Orig. Price: $23 • **Value: $23**

⑨

Auntie Alice
10" • #9183 • TJ
Issued: 1993 • Retired: 1996
Orig. Price: $21 • **Value: $46**

BEARS

	Price Paid	Value Of My Collection
1.		
2.		
3.		
4.		
5.		
6.		
7.		
8.		
9.		

✏ PENCIL TOTALS

①

Auntie Bearburg
info unavailable
Orig. Price: N/A • **Value: N/E**

②

Auntie Erma
10" • #91832 • TJ
Issued: 1996 • Retired: 1997
Orig. Price: $21 • **Value: $34**

③

Auntie Iola
10" • #91612 • TJ
Issued: 1995 • Retired: 1997
Orig. Price: $30 • **Value: $45**

④

Avery B. Bean
14" • #5101 • JB
Issued: pre-1990 • Retired: 1990
Orig. Price: N/A • **Value: $165**

⑤

Baaah'b
8" • #9131 • TJ
Issued: 1995 • Retired: 1997
Orig. Price: $17 • **Value: $36**

⑥

Baby
10" • #6105B • TJ
Issued: 1990 • Retired: 1991
Orig. Price: N/A • **Value: $285**

⑦

Bailey *(Fall 1992)*
8" • #9199 • TJ
Issued: 1992 • Retired: 1993
Orig. Price: N/A • **Value: $700**

⑧

Bailey *(Spring 1993)*
8" • N/A • TJ
Issued: 1993 • Retired: 1994
Orig. Price: N/A • **Value: $350**

⑨

Bailey *(Fall 1993)*
8" • #9170 • TJ
Issued: 1993 • Retired: 1994
Orig. Price: N/A • **Value: $300**

⑩

Bailey *(Spring 1994)*
8" • #9199-01 • TJ
Issued: 1994 • Retired: 1995
Orig. Price: $26 • **Value: $140**

BEARS

	Price Paid	Value Of My Collection
1.		
2.		
3.		
4.		
5.		
6.		
7.		
8.		
9.		
10.		

✏ PENCIL TOTALS

(1)

Bailey *(Fall 1994)*
8" • #9199-02 • TJ
Issued: 1994 • Retired: 1995
Orig. Price: $26 • **Value: $68**

(2)

Bailey *(Spring 1995)*
8" • #9199-03 • TJ
Issued: 1995 • Retired: 1996
Orig. Price: $26 • **Value: $57**

(3)

Bailey *(Fall 1995)*
8" • #9199-04 • TJ
Issued: 1995 • Retired: 1996
Orig. Price: $24 • **Value: $52**

(4)

Bailey *(Spring 1996)*
8" • #9199-05 • TJ
Issued: 1996 • Retired: 1997
Orig. Price: $26 • **Value: $48**

(5)

Bailey *(Fall 1996)*
8" • #9199-06 • TJ
Issued: 1996 • Retired: 1997
Orig. Price: $26 • **Value: $44**

(6)

Bailey *(Spring 1997)*
8" • #9199-07 • TJ
Issued: 1997 • Retired: 1998
Orig. Price: $27 • **Value: $40**

BEARS

	Price Paid	Value Of My Collection
1.		
2.		
3.		
4.		
5.		
6.		
7.		
8.		
9.		
10.		

✏ PENCIL TOTALS

(7)

Bailey *(Fall 1997)*
8" • #9199-08 • TJ
Issued: 1997 • Retired: 1998
Orig. Price: $27 • **Value: $35**

(8)

Bailey *(Spring 1998)*
8" • #9199-09 • TJ
Issued: 1998 • To Be Retired: 1999
Orig. Price: $27 • **Value: $27**

(9)

Bailey *(Fall 1998)*
8" • #9199-10 • TJ
Issued: 1998 • To Be Retired: 1999
Orig. Price: $27 • **Value: $27**

(10)
New!

Bailey *(Spring 1999)*
8" • #9199-11 • TJ
Issued: 1999 • Current
Orig. Price: $27 • **Value: $27**

1

Bailey & Matthew
(w/resin ornaments, *Fall 1996*)
N/A • #9224 • TJ
Issued: 1996 • Retired: 1996
Orig. Price: $70 • **Value: $90**

2

Bailey & Matthew
(w/resin ornaments, *Fall 1997*)
N/A • #9225 • TJ
Issued: 1997 • Retired: 1997
Orig. Price: $70 • **Value: $90**

3

Bailey & Matthew
(w/resin ornaments, *Fall 1998)*
N/A • #9227 • TJ
Issued: 1998 • Retired: 1998
Orig. Price: $71 • **Value: $78**

4

Baldwin
5.5" • #5718 • AS
Issued: 1992 • Current
Orig. Price: $7 • **Value: $7**

5

Barnaby B. Bean
10" • #5150-03 • JB
Issued: 1994 • To Be Retired: 1999
Orig. Price: $16 • **Value: $16**

6

Bartholemew B. Bean
10" • #5103 • JB
Issued: 1992 • Retired: 1998
Orig. Price: $14 • **Value: $25**

7

Baxter B. Bean
8" • #5151-05 • JB
Issued: 1994 • To Be Retired: 1999
Orig. Price: $12 • **Value: $13**

8

Bea Bear
info unavailable
Orig. Price: N/A • **Value: N/E**

9

Bear-Among-Bears
16" • #5050 • N/A
Issued: pre-1990 • Retired: N/A
Orig. Price: N/A • **Value: N/E**

10

Bear-Among-Bears
16" • #5051 • N/A
Issued: pre-1990 • Retired: N/A
Orig. Price: N/A • **Value: N/E**

BEARS		
	Price Paid	Value Of My Collection
1.		
2.		
3.		
4.		
5.		
6.		
7.		
8.		
9.		
10.		
✎ PENCIL TOTALS		

(1)

Bear-Among-Bears
info unavailable
Orig. Price: N/A • **Value: N/E**

(2)

Bear-Let
8" • #5020 • WB
Issued: pre-1990 • Retired: 1992
Orig. Price: $9 • **Value: $120**

(3)

Bear-Let
8" • #5021 • N/A
Issued: pre-1990 • Retired: N/A
Orig. Price: N/A • **Value: N/E**

(4)

Bearly-A-Bear
10" • #5030 • WB
Issued: pre-1990 • Retired: 1992
Orig. Price: $13 • **Value: $115**

(5)

Bearly-A-Bear
10" • #5031 • WB
Issued: pre-1990 • Retired: 1991
Orig. Price: $13 • **Value: $130**

(6)

Bears' Bear
12" • #5040 • WB
Issued: pre-1990 • Retired: 1992
Orig. Price: $18 • **Value: $270**

BEARS

	Price Paid	Value Of My Collection
1.		
2.		
3.		
4.		
5.		
6.		
7.		
8.		
9.		

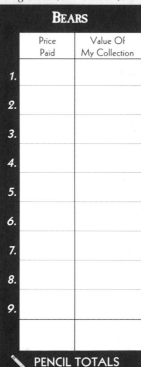

PENCIL TOTALS

(7)

Bears' Bear
12" • #5041 • WB
Issued: pre-1990 • Retired: 1992
Orig. Price: $18 • **Value: $250**

(8)

Beatrice
14" • #6168 • TJ
Issued: 1991 • Retired: 1991
Orig. Price: $63 • **Value: $435**

(9)

Becky
6" • #91395 • TJ
Issued: 1995 • Current
Orig. Price: $11 • **Value: $12**

54

BEARS

① 

Becky
6" • #91395-01 • TJ
Issued: 1996 • To Be Retired: 1999
Orig. Price: $11 • **Value: $12**

② 

Bedford B. Bean
10" • #5121-08 • JB
Issued: 1996 • Retired: 1996
Orig. Price: $14 • **Value: $60**

③ 

PHOTO
UNAVAILABLE

Benjamin
10" • #9159 • TJ
Issued: 1993 • Retired: 1994
Orig. Price: $20 • **Value: $46**

④ 

Berrybear
14" • #5762 • HD
Issued: 1992 • Retired: 1994
Orig. Price: $27 • **Value: N/E**

⑤ New!

Bethany Thistlebeary
6" • #913955 • TJ
Issued: 1999 • Current
Orig. Price: $13 • **Value: $13**

⑥ 

Betsey
6" • #913952 • TJ
Issued: 1997 • Current
Orig. Price: $13 • **Value: $13**

⑦ 

Bianca T. Witebred
8" • #912076 • TJ
Issued: 1998 • Current
Orig. Price: $19 • **Value: $19**

⑧ 

Big Boy
5.5" • #9108 • TJ
Issued: 1995 • Retired: 1997
Orig. Price: $12 • **Value: $43**

⑨ 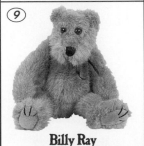

Billy Ray
9" • #5850 • BB
Issued: 1992 • Retired: 1997
Orig. Price: $14 • **Value: $32**

	BEARS	
	Price Paid	Value Of My Collection
1.		
2.		
3.		
4.		
5.		
6.		
7.		
8.		
9.		
✏ PENCIL TOTALS		

①

Binkie B. Bear
16" • #5115 • JB
Issued: pre-1990 • Retired: 1993
Orig. Price: $27 • **Value: $105**

②

Binkie B. Bear II
16" • #5115 • JB
Issued: 1994 • Retired: 1996
Orig. Price: $27 • **Value: $73**

③ New!

Bixby Trufflebeary
12" • #56390-10 • BA
Issued: 1999 • Current
Orig. Price: $16 • **Value: $16**

④

Blackstone
6" • #5840-07 • GB
Issued: 1997 • Current
Orig. Price: $9 • **Value: $9**

⑤

Blanche de Bearvoire
6" • #91841 • TJ
Issued: 1996 • Retired: 1998
Orig. Price: $9 • **Value: $18**

⑥

Blinkin
18" • #5807 • SB
Issued: 1991 • Retired: 1992
Orig. Price: $32 • **Value: $195**

BEARS

	Price Paid	Value Of My Collection
1.		
2.		
3.		
4.		
5.		
6.		
7.		
8.		
9.		
10.		

✏ PENCIL TOTALS

⑦

Bluebeary
8" • #56421-06 • BA
Issued: 1998 • Current
Orig. Price: $11 • **Value: $11**

⑧

Bobbie Jo
12" • #5853 • BB
Issued: 1992 • Retired: 1997
Orig. Price: $20 • **Value: $46**

⑨

Bonnie
6" • #913951 • TJ
Issued: 1997 • Current
Orig. Price: $13 • **Value: $13**

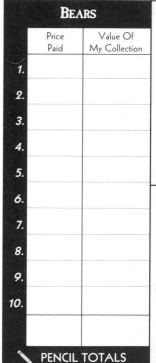

⑩

Boris Berriman
6" • #918021 • TJ
Issued: 1998 • Current
Orig. Price: $12 • **Value: $12**

BEARS

①

Bosley
8.5" • #91561 • TJ
Issued: 1997 • To Be Retired: 1999
Orig. Price: $12 • **Value: $12**

②

Bradley Boobear
8" • #919610 • TJ
Issued: 1998 • Current
Orig. Price: $13 • **Value: $13**

③ New!

Bradshaw P. Beansford
14" • #51091-08 • JB
Issued: 1999 • Current
Orig. Price: $20 • **Value: $20**

④

Braxton B. Bear
14" • #51081-08 • JB
Issued: 1998 • Current
Orig. Price: $20 • **Value: $20**

⑤

Brewin
10" • #5802 • SB
Issued: 1992 • Retired: 1995
Orig. Price: $20 • **Value: $70**

⑥

Brewin
10" • #5806 • SB
Issued: 1991 • Retired: 1991
Orig. Price: N/A • **Value: $70**

⑦

Bromley Q. Bear
8" • #5151-03 • JB
Issued: 1998 • Current
Orig. Price: $13 • **Value: $13**

⑧

Bruce
8" • #1000-08 • CC
Issued: 1993 • Current
Orig. Price: $6 • **Value: $6**

⑨

Bruce
8" • #9157-08 • TJ
Issued: 1993 • Retired: 1994
Orig. Price: $14 • **Value: $56**

⑩

Bruce
8" • #98038 • TJ
Issued: 1996 • Retired: 1997
Orig. Price: $13 • **Value: $32**

	BEARS	
	Price Paid	Value Of My Collection
1.		
2.		
3.		
4.		
5.		
6.		
7.		
8.		
9.		
10.		
	PENCIL TOTALS	

Bruinhilda Von Bruin
6" • #5010-03 • WB
Issued: 1994 • Retired: 1995
Orig. Price: $12 • **Value: $44**

Bubba
16" • #5856 • BB
Issued: 1992 • Retired: 1997
Orig. Price: $27 • **Value: $50**

Buckingham
21" • #57221 • AS
Issued: 1997 • Current
Orig. Price: $55 • **Value: $55**

Buckley
8" • #9104 • TJ
Issued: 1995 • Retired: 1996
Orig. Price: $16 • **Value: $54**

Buffington Fitzbruin
10" • #912031 • TJ
Issued: 1997 • Retired: 1998
Orig. Price: $20 • **Value: $27**

Buffy
12" • #5639-10 • BA
Issued: 1995 • Retired: 1996
Orig. Price: $16 • **Value: $45**

BEARS

	Price Paid	Value Of My Collection
1.		
2.		
3.		
4.		
5.		
6.		
7.		
8.		
9.		

✎ PENCIL TOTALS

New!

Bumbershoot B. Jodibear
8" • #92000-03 • TJ
Issued: 1999 • Current
Orig. Price: $20 • **Value: $20**

Burke P. Bear
14" • #5109-05 • JB
Issued: 1997 • Current
Orig. Price: $20 • **Value: $20**

Burl
10" • #91761 • TJ
Issued: 1996 • Retired: 1998
Orig. Price: $20 • **Value: $28**

BEARS

(1)

New!

Buttercup C. Snicklefritz
9" • #51760-12 • BY
Issued: 1999 • Current
Orig. Price: $12 • **Value: $12**

(2)

Buzz B. Bean
10" • #5120 • JB
Issued: pre-1990 • Retired: 1990
Orig. Price: N/A • **Value: $190**

(3)

Buzzby
8" • #9143 • TJ
Issued: 1994 • Retired: 1995
Orig. Price: $18 • **Value: $53**

(4)

PHOTO UNAVAILABLE

Cabin Bear
info unavailable
Orig. Price: N/A • **Value: N/E**

(5)

Cagney
8" • #9189-01 • TJ
Issued: 1994 • Retired: 1996
Orig. Price: $20 • **Value: $50**

(6)

Caledonia
6" • #5840-01 • GB
Issued: 1997 • Current
Orig. Price: $9 • **Value: $9**

(7)

Callaghan
8" • #5704 • AS
Issued: 1990 • Retired: 1996
Orig. Price: $12 • **Value: $52**

(8)

Calvin Ellis
8" • #91223 • TJ
Issued: 1996 • Retired: 1997
Orig. Price: $18 • **Value: $33**

(9)

Camille du Bear
6" • #91804 • TJ
Issued: 1996 • Retired: 1998
Orig. Price: $9 • **Value: $20**

(10)

Canute
6" • #9136 • TJ
Issued: 1994 • Retired: 1996
Orig. Price: $12 • **Value: $39**

BEARS

	Price Paid	Value Of My Collection
1.		
2.		
3.		
4.		
5.		
6.		
7.		
8.		
9.		
10.		

PENCIL TOTALS

① New!

Carmella de Bearvoire
6" • #918401 • TJ
Issued: 1999 • Current
Orig. Price: $9 • **Value: $9**

②

Carter M. Bearington
10" • #590050-08 • MB
Issued: 1998 • Retired: 1998
Orig. Price: $31 • **Value: $52**

③

Cavendish
12" • #5701-02 • AS
Issued: 1994 • Retired: 1996
Orig. Price: $20 • **Value: $46**

④

Cecil
5.5" • #5726 • AS
Issued: 1993 • Retired: 1996
Orig. Price: $7 • **Value: $25**

⑤

Chamberlain
16" • #5709 • AS
Issued: 1990 • Retired: 1992
Orig. Price: $32 • **Value: $145**

⑥

Chamomille Q. Quignapple
10" • #91004 • TJ
Issued: 1997 • Current
Orig. Price: $24 • **Value: $24**

BEARS

	Price Paid	Value Of My Collection
1.		
2.		
3.		
4.		
5.		
6.		
7.		
8.		
9.		
10.		

✏ PENCIL TOTALS

⑦

Chan
6" • #9153 • TJ
Issued: 1994 • Retired: 1998
Orig. Price: $12 • **Value: $25**

⑧

Chanel de la Plumtete
6" • #9184 • TJ
Issued: 1995 • Current
Orig. Price: $9 • **Value: $9**

⑨

Chauncey Fitzbruin
6" • #912033 • TJ
Issued: 1997 • Current
Orig. Price: $12 • **Value: $12**

⑩

Chipper
8" • #5642-05 • BA
Issued: 1996 • Retired: 1997
Orig. Price: $11 • **Value: $22**

(1)

Christian
8" • #9190 • TJ
Issued: 1992 • Current
Orig. Price: $18 • **Value: $18**

(2)

PHOTO UNAVAILABLE

Christmas Bear
info unavailable
Orig. Price: N/A • **Value: N/E**

(3)

Christopher
10" • #9161 • TJ
Issued: 1993 • Retired: 1998
Orig. Price: $20 • **Value: $29**

(4)

Churchill
12" • #5700 • AS
Issued: 1990 • Current
Orig. Price: $20 • **Value: $20**

(5)

Claire
10" • #9179 • TJ
Issued: 1994 • Retired: 1998
Orig. Price: $20 • **Value: $28**

(6)

Clara
14" • #911061 • TJ
Issued: 1996 • Retired: 1998
Orig. Price: $20 • **Value: $30**

(7)

Clarissa
16" • #91202 • TJ
Issued: 1996 • Current
Orig. Price: $58 • **Value: $58**

(8)

Cleason
10" • #5121N • JB
Issued: 1992 • Retired: 1996
Orig. Price: $14 • **Value: $33**

(9)

Clement
16" • #5710 • AS
Issued: 1990 • Retired: 1992
Orig. Price: $32 • **Value: $135**

(10)

Clementine
6" • #913953 • TJ
Issued: 1998 • Current
Orig. Price: $12 • **Value: $12**

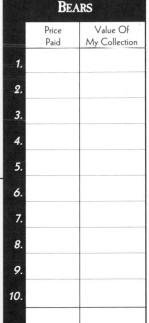

	Price Paid	Value Of My Collection
1.		
2.		
3.		
4.		
5.		
6.		
7.		
8.		
9.		
10.		

BEARS

✏ PENCIL TOTALS

① Clinton B. Bean
14" • #5109 • JB
Issued: 1993 • Retired: 1998
Orig. Price: $20 • **Value: $30**

New!

② Clover L. Buzzoff
10" • #91772 • TJ
Issued: 1999 • Current
Orig. Price: $18 • **Value: $18**

③ Coco
10" • #5121 • JB
Issued: 1991 • Retired: 1995
Orig. Price: $14 • **Value: $45**

④ Colleen O'Bruin
6" • #91805 • TJ
Issued: 1995 • Retired: 1997
Orig. Price: $12 • **Value: $28**

⑤ Constance
16" • #91202-01 • TJ
Issued: 1998 • Current
Orig. Price: $48 • **Value: $48**

⑥ Corinna
16" • #91201 • TJ
Issued: 1996 • Current
Orig. Price: $45 • **Value: $45**

BEARS

	Price Paid	Value Of My Collection
1.		
2.		
3.		
4.		
5.		
6.		
7.		
8.		
9.		

✎ PENCIL TOTALS

⑦ Corinna II
16" • #912011 • TJ
Issued: 1997 • Retired: 1998
Orig. Price: $45 • **Value: $50**

⑧ Cornwallis
16" • #9126 • TJ
Issued: 1994 • Retired: 1996
Orig. Price: $45 • **Value: $75**

⑨ Cornwallis
16" • #9126-01 • TJ
Issued: 1996 • Retired: 1997
Orig. Price: $53 • **Value: $66**

BEARS

① Courtney
16" • #912021 • TJ
Issued: 1997 • Current
Orig. Price: $45 • **Value: $45**

② Craxton B. Bean
10" • #510300-11 • JB
Issued: 1998 • Current
Orig. Price: $14 • **Value: $14**

③ Daryl Bear
16" • #5114 • JB
Issued: pre-1990 • Retired: 1993
Orig. Price: $27 • **Value: $115**

④ Delaney And The Duffer (LE-500)
N/A • N/A • N/A
Issued: 1993 • Retired: 1994
Orig. Price: $74 • **Value: $200**

⑤ New!
Delanie B. Beansford
16" • #51101-10 • JB
Issued: 1999 • Current
Orig. Price: $29 • **Value: $29**

⑥ Delbert Quignapple
10" • #91003 • TJ
Issued: 1996 • Current
Orig. Price: $24 • **Value: $24**

⑦ Delmarva V. Crackenpot
10" • #91002 • TJ
Issued: 1997 • To Be Retired: 1999
Orig. Price: $29 • **Value: $29**

⑧ Desdemona T. Witebred
10" • #912075 • TJ
Issued: 1997 • Retired: 1998
Orig. Price: $21 • **Value: $30**

⑨ Dewey P. Wongbruin
16" • #5154 • JB
Issued: 1997 • Current
Orig. Price: $29 • **Value: $29**

⑩ Dexter
8" • #91331 • TJ
Issued: 1996 • Retired: 1998
Orig. Price: $25 • **Value: $32**

BEARS	Price Paid	Value Of My Collection
1.		
2.		
3.		
4.		
5.		
6.		
7.		
8.		
9.		
10.		
PENCIL TOTALS		

①

Diana (w/boy cub)
info unavailable
Orig. Price: N/A • **Value: N/E**

②

Diana (w/girl cub)
info unavailable
Orig. Price: N/A • **Value: N/E**

③

New!

Dilly McDoodle
9" • #51710-12 • BY
Issued: 1999 • Current
Orig. Price: $8 • **Value: $8**

④

Dink
16" • #5641 • BA
Issued: 1992 • Retired: 1994
Orig. Price: $21 • **Value: $42**

⑤

Dink
16" • #5641-08 • BA
Issued: 1995 • Retired: 1997
Orig. Price: $24 • **Value: $28**

⑥

Disreali
5.5" • #5716 • AS
Issued: 1991 • Retired: 1993
Orig. Price: $7 • **Value: $66**

BEARS

	Price Paid	Value Of My Collection
1.		
2.		
3.		
4.		
5.		
6.		
7.		
8.		
9.		
10.		

✏ PENCIL TOTALS

⑦

Dufus Bear
16" • #5112 • JB
Issued: pre-1990 • Retired: 1997
Orig. Price: $27 • **Value: $45**

⑧

Eddie Beanberger
(formerly "Eddie Beanbauer")
10" • #9119 • TJ
Issued: 1995 • Current
Orig. Price: $27 • **Value: $27**

⑨

Eddie Beanberger
10" • #9119-01 • TJ
Issued: 1996 • Retired: 1997
Orig. Price: $30 • **Value: $45**

⑩

Eden
5.5" • #5708 • AS
Issued: 1990 • Retired: 1996
Orig. Price: $7 • **Value: $26**

BEARS

1

Eden
6" • #9139 • TJ
Issued: 1994 • Retired: 1996
Orig. Price: $13 • **Value: $40**

2

Eden II
6" • #91391 • TJ
Issued: 1996 • Retired: 1997
Orig. Price: $13 • **Value: $25**

3

Edmund (Fall 1993)
8" • #9175 • TJ
Issued: 1993 • Retired: 1994
Orig. Price: N/A • **Value: $215**

4

Edmund (Spring 1994)
8" • #9175-01 • TJ
Issued: 1994 • Retired: 1995
Orig. Price: $26 • **Value: $130**
Variation: black & white shirt
Value: $188

5

Edmund (Fall 1994)
8" • #9175-02 • TJ
Issued: 1994 • Retired: 1995
Orig. Price: $24 • **Value: $100**

6

Edmund (Spring 1995)
8" • #9175-03 • TJ
Issued: 1995 • Retired: 1996
Orig. Price: $24 • **Value: $50**

7

Edmund (Fall 1995)
8" • #9175-04 • TJ
Issued: 1995 • Retired: 1996
Orig. Price: $24 • **Value: $47**

8

Edmund (Spring 1996)
8" • #9175-05 • TJ
Issued: 1996 • Retired: 1997
Orig. Price: $26 • **Value: $42**

9

Edmund (Fall 1996)
8" • #9175-06 • TJ
Issued: 1996 • Retired: 1997
Orig. Price: $24 • **Value: $40**

10

Edmund (Spring 1997)
8" • #9175-07 • TJ
Issued: 1997 • Retired: 1998
Orig. Price: $24 • **Value: $38**

BEARS

	Price Paid	Value Of My Collection
1.		
2.		
3.		
4.		
5.		
6.		
7.		
8.		
9.		
10.		

✎ PENCIL TOTALS

①	②	③

Edmund *(Fall 1997)*
8" • #9175-08 • TJ
Issued: 1997 • Retired: 1998
Orig. Price: $24 • **Value: $32**

Edmund *(Spring 1998)*
8" • #9175-09 • TJ
Issued: 1998 • To Be Retired: 1999
Orig. Price: $26 • **Value: $26**

Edmund *(Fall 1998)*
8" • #9175-10 • TJ
Issued: 1998 • To Be Retired: 1999
Orig. Price: $27 • **Value: $27**

④ New!

⑤

⑥
PHOTO UNAVAILABLE

Edmund *(Spring 1999)*
8" • #9175-11 • TJ
Issued: 1999 • Current
Orig. Price: $26 • **Value: $26**

Eldora
14" • #91615 • TJ
Issued: 1996 • Retired: 1998
Orig. Price: $31 • **Value: $38**

Eleanor Bear (set/3,
Eleanor, baby and chair)
N/A • #6102 • TJ
Issued: 1990 • Retired: 1990
Orig. Price: N/A • **Value: $575**

BEARS

	Price Paid	Value Of My Collection
1.		
2.		
3.		
4.		
5.		
6.		
7.		
8.		
9.		
10.		

✏ **PENCIL TOTALS**

⑦

⑧

Elgin
6.5" • #9129 • TJ
Issued: 1994 • Retired: 1997
Orig. Price: $12 • **Value: $25**

Elliot B. Bean
14" • #5108 • JB
Issued: pre-1990 • Retired: 1998
Orig. Price: $20 • **Value: $30**

⑨

⑩

Elly Mae
9" • #5850-10 • BB
Issued: 1995 • Retired: 1997
Orig. Price: $14 • **Value: $32**

Elmore Flatski
8" • #5680-08 • FL
Issued: 1995 • Retired: 1997
Orig. Price: $13 • **Value: $26**

BEARS

Elsworth
12" • #1107-05 • CC
Issued: 1997 • Current
Orig. Price: $12 • **Value: $12**

Elton Elfberg
10" • #917306 • TJ
Issued: 1997 • Retired: 1998
Orig. Price: $21 • **Value: $30**

Elvin Q. Elfberg
10" • #917301 • TJ
Issued: 1997 • Current
Orig. Price: $25 • **Value: $25**

Emma
14" • #9101 • TJ
Issued: 1995 • Retired: 1997
Orig. Price: $27 • **Value: $50**

Emmett Elfberg
10" • #917305 • TJ
Issued: 1996 • To Be Retired: 1999
Orig. Price: $21 • **Value: $21**

Emmy Lou
10" • #91001 • TJ
Issued: 1996 • To Be Retired: 1999
Orig. Price: $24 • **Value: $24**

Erin K. Bear
7" • #91562 • TJ
Issued: 1996 • Retired: 1998
Orig. Price: $11 • **Value: $19**

Essex
12" • #5701-10 • AS
Issued: 1994 • Retired: 1996
Orig. Price: $20 • **Value: $45**

Ethan
9" • #917322 • TJ
Issued: 1998 • To Be Retired: 1999
Orig. Price: $21 • **Value: $21**

Ethel B. Bruin
12" • #912051 • TJ
Issued: 1997 • Retired: 1998
Orig. Price: $25 • **Value: $36**

BEARS

	Price Paid	Value Of My Collection
1.		
2.		
3.		
4.		
5.		
6.		
7.		
8.		
9.		
10.		

PENCIL TOTALS

(1)

Eudemia Q. Quignapple
9" • #91006 • TJ
Issued: 1997 • Current
Orig. Price: $16 • **Value: $16**

(2)

Eugenia
16" • #9120 • TJ
Issued: 1994 • Retired: 1996
Orig. Price: $45 • **Value: $84**

(3)

Eugenia The Apple Seller
16" • #9120-01 • AS
Issued: 1995 • Retired: 1995
Orig. Price: $53 • **Value: $125**

(4)

Eunice P. Snowbeary
9" • #9137-01 • TJ
Issued: 1997 • Current
Orig. Price: $20 • **Value: $20**

(5)

Evelyn
10" • #91614 • TJ
Issued: 1997 • Retired: 1998
Orig. Price: $24 • **Value: $29**

(6)

Everest
8.5" • #5844-05 • GB
Issued: 1996 • Current
Orig. Price: $17 • **Value: $17**

BEARS

	Price Paid	Value Of My Collection
1.		
2.		
3.		
4.		
5.		
6.		
7.		
8.		
9.		
10.		

PENCIL TOTALS

(7)

Ewell
8" • #9127 • TJ
Issued: 1994 • Current
Orig. Price: $17 • **Value: $17**

(8)

Father Chrisbear
info unavailable
Orig. Price: N/A • **Value: $170**

(9)

PHOTO UNAVAILABLE

Father Christmas
info unavailable
Orig. Price: N/A • **Value: N/E**

(10)

Father Christmas
info unavailable
Orig. Price: N/A • **Value: N/E**

BEARS

①

Federico
11" • #1100-08 • CC
Issued: 1993 • Retired: 1997
Orig. Price: $10 • **Value: $28**

②

Federico
11" • #98039 • TJ
Issued: 1996 • Retired: 1997
Orig. Price: $21 • **Value: $45**

③

Felicity S. Elfberg
5.5" • #917300 • TJ
Issued: 1997 • Retired: 1998
Orig. Price: $13 • **Value: $19**

④

Fidelity B. Morgan IV
17" • #5110-05 • JB
Issued: 1997 • Current
Orig. Price: $29 • **Value: $29**

⑤

Fiona Fitzbruin
14" • #91203 • TJ
Issued: 1997 • Retired: 1998
Orig. Price: $26 • **Value: $30**

⑥

Fitzgerald D. Bearington
12" • #590040-03 • MB
Issued: 1997 • Retired: 1997
Orig. Price: $48 • **Value: $65**

⑦

Fitzgerald O'Bruin
6" • #91802 • TJ
Issued: 1995 • Retired: 1997
Orig. Price: $12 • **Value: $28**

⑧

Fitzroy
N/A • #5795 • TJ
Issued: 1992 • Retired: 1992
Orig. Price: $18 • **Value: $72**

⑨

Fitzroy
7.5" • #9195 • TJ
Issued: 1992 • Retired: 1994
Orig. Price: $16 • **Value: N/E**

⑩

Fleurette
12" • #6103B • AS
Issued: 1991 • Retired: 1991
Orig. Price: N/A • **Value: N/E**

	Price Paid	Value Of My Collection
BEARS		
1.		
2.		
3.		
4.		
5.		
6.		
7.		
8.		
9.		
10.		
✏ PENCIL TOTALS		

①

Floyd
9" • #917321 • TJ
Issued: 1998 • Current
Orig. Price: $21 • **Value: $21**

② New!

Forrest B. Bearsley
10" • #91744 • TJ
Issued: 1999 • Current
Orig. Price: $20 • **Value: $20**

③

Franklin
8" • #1050-06 • DB
Issued: 1995 • Retired: 1996
Orig. Price: $11 • **Value: $54**

④

Franz Von Bruin
6" • #5010-06 • WB
Issued: 1994 • Retired: 1995
Orig. Price: $10 • **Value: $49**

⑤

Freddy Beanberger
10" • #911901 • TJ
Issued: 1998 • Retired: 1998
Orig. Price: $27 • **Value: $32**

⑥

Gabriel
9" • #5825 • CB
Issued: 1991 • Retired: 1997
Orig. Price: $14 • **Value: $45**

BEARS

	Price Paid	Value Of My Collection
1.		
2.		
3.		
4.		
5.		
6.		
7.		
8.		
9.		
10.		

✏ PENCIL TOTALS

⑦
PHOTO
UNAVAILABLE

Gardner
N/A • #6162B • TJ
Issued: 1991 • Retired: 1991
Orig. Price: $63 • **Value: N/E**

⑧

Geneva
8" • #9162 • TJ
Issued: 1994 • Retired: 1994
Orig. Price: $18 • **Value: $118**

⑨

George
11" • #1100-03 • CC
Issued: 1996 • Retired: 1997
Orig. Price: $10 • **Value: $25**

⑩

Geraldo
8" • #912441 • TJ
Issued: 1996 • Retired: 1997
Orig. Price: $19 • **Value: $34**

BEARS

①

Gladstone
12" • #5701 • AS
Issued: 1990 • Retired: 1993
Orig. Price: $20 • **Value: $82**

②

Glenda
12" • #91891-04 • TJ
Issued: 1998 • Current
Orig. Price: $21 • **Value: $21**

③

Glynnis
8" • #918910-02 • TJ
Issued: 1998 • Current
Orig. Price: $17 • **Value: $17**

④

Gorden B. Bean
10" • #5105 • JB
Issued: pre-1990 • Retired: 1998
Orig. Price: $14 • **Value: $26**

⑤

PHOTO UNAVAILABLE

Grace
N/A • #6163B • TJ
Issued: 1991 • Retired: 1991
Orig. Price: $63 • **Value: N/E**

⑥

Grace
10" • #91742 • TJ
Issued: 1997 • Retired: 1998
Orig. Price: $20 • **Value: $25**

⑦

Gram
18" • #5775 • HD
Issued: 1991 • Retired: 1991
Orig. Price: $39 • **Value: $280**

⑧

Gramps
18" • #5770 • HD
Issued: 1991 • Retired: 1991
Orig. Price: $39 • **Value: $300**

⑨

PHOTO UNAVAILABLE

Grandma Bearburg
14" • N/A • N/A
Issued: 1992 • Retired: 1992
Orig. Price: N/A • **Value: N/E**

⑩

Grenville
16" • #5715 • AS
Issued: 1992 • Current
Orig. Price: $32 • **Value: $32**

BEARS

	Price Paid	Value Of My Collection
1.		
2.		
3.		
4.		
5.		
6.		
7.		
8.		
9.		
10.		
✎ PENCIL TOTALS		

Grover
8" • #91739 • TJ
Issued: 1997 • Retired: 1998
Orig. Price: $12 • **Value: $18**

Grumps
9" • #5766 • HD
Issued: 1991 • Retired: 1994
Orig. Price: $14 • **Value: $76**

Guinevere
12" • #91891-09 • TJ
Issued: 1996 • Current
Orig. Price: $21 • **Value: $21**

Gunnar
8" • #9123 • TJ
Issued: 1995 • Retired: 1996
Orig. Price: $24 • **Value: $40**

Gunther Von Bruin
6" • #5012 • WB
Issued: 1993 • Retired: 1994
Orig. Price: N/A • **Value: $88**

Gustav Von Bruin
10" • #5011 • WB
Issued: 1993 • Retired: 1994
Orig. Price: $21 • **Value: $58**

BEARS

	Price Paid	Value Of My Collection
1.		
2.		
3.		
4.		
5.		
6.		
7.		
8.		
9.		
10.		

✎ PENCIL TOTALS

Gwain
12" • #91891-06 • TJ
Issued: 1997 • Current
Orig. Price: $21 • **Value: $21**

New!

Gwendina
11" • #91891-12 • TJ
Issued: 1999 • Current
Orig. Price: $21 • **Value: $21**

Gwendolyn
12" • #91891-02 • TJ
Issued: 1997 • Current
Orig. Price: $21 • **Value: $21**

Gwinton
8" • #918910-06 • TJ
Issued: 1998 • Current
Orig. Price: $17 • **Value: $17**

BEARS

(1)

Gwynda
8" • #918910-09 • TJ
Issued: 1998 • Current
Orig. Price: $17 • **Value: $17**

(2)

Hadley Flatski
8" • #5680-05 • FL
Issued: 1994 • Retired: 1997
Orig. Price: $12 • **Value: $35**

(3)

Hancock
8" • #1050-11 • DB
Issued: 1995 • Retired: 1996
Orig. Price: $11 • **Value: $41**

(4)

Hans Q. Berriman
6" • #91392 • TJ
Issued: 1997 • Current
Orig. Price: $13 • **Value: $13**

(5)

Harding
8" • #1051-06 • DB
Issued: 1996 • Retired: 1998
Orig. Price: $13 • **Value: $25**

(6) New!

Harding G. Bearington
10" • #590051-01 • MB
Issued: 1999 • To Be Retired: 1999
Orig. Price: $28 • **Value: $28**

(7)

Harrison
10" • #9176 • TJ
Issued: 1993 • Retired: 1997
Orig. Price: $20 • **Value: $34**

(8) New!

Hartley B. Mine
8.5" • #91521 • TJ
Issued: 1999 • Current
Orig. Price: $14 • **Value: $14**

(9)

 PHOTO UNAVAILABLE

Hattie & Annie
info unavailable
Orig. Price: N/A • **Value: N/E**

(10)

Hawley Flatski
8" • #56801-03 • FL
Issued: 1998 • Current
Orig. Price: $13 • **Value: $13**

BEARS		
	Price Paid	Value Of My Collection
1.		
2.		
3.		
4.		
5.		
6.		
7.		
8.		
9.		
10.		
✏ PENCIL TOTALS		

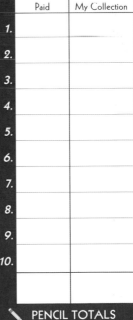

(1)

Hazel
8" • #1000-03 • CC
Issued: 1993 • Retired: 1996
Orig. Price: $6 • **Value: $35**

(2)

Heath
10" • #5703 • AS
Issued: 1990 • Retired: 1992
Orig. Price: $18 • **Value: $82**

(3)

Heath II
10" • #5703N • AS
Issued: 1992 • Retired: 1997
Orig. Price: $18 • **Value: $32**

(4) New!

Hemingway K. Grizzman
14" • #91263 • TJ
Issued: 1999 • Current
Orig. Price: $40 • **Value: $40**

(5) New!

Henley Fitzhampton
6" • #912034 • TJ
Issued: 1999 • Current
Orig. Price: $13 • **Value: $13**

(6)

Henry
8" • #1000-05 • CC
Issued: 1993 • Retired: 1995
Orig. Price: $6 • **Value: $43**

BEARS

	Price Paid	Value Of My Collection
1.		
2.		
3.		
4.		
5.		
6.		
7.		
8.		
9.		
10.		

✏ PENCIL TOTALS

(7)

Henson
10" • #58011-05 • SB
Issued: 1998 • Current
Orig. Price: $20 • **Value: $20**

(8)

Hermine Grisslin
16" • #91206 • TJ
Issued: 1995 • Retired: 1997
Orig. Price: $45 • **Value: $54**

(9)

Hershal
16" • #5125 • JB
Issued: 1991 • Retired: 1992
Orig. Price: $27 • **Value: $140**

(10)

Hillary B. Bean
14" • #5123-10 • JB
Issued: 1993 • Retired: 1998
Orig. Price: $20 • **Value: $30**

(1)

Hockley
16" • #5640 • BA
Issued: 1992 • Retired: 1996
Orig. Price: $21 • **Value: $50**

(2)

Homer
14" • #5760 • HD
Issued: 1991 • Retired: 1994
Orig. Price: $27 • **Value: $170**

(3)

PHOTO UNAVAILABLE

Homer
N/A • #6166B • TJ
Issued: 1991 • Retired: 1991
Orig. Price: $63 • **Value: $170**

(4)

Homer
8" • #9177 • TJ
Issued: 1993 • Retired: 1996
Orig. Price: $26 • **Value: $52**

(5)
New!

Honey P. Snicklefritz (musical)
8" • #51760-08 • BY
Issued: 1999 • Current
Orig. Price: $12 • **Value: $12**

(6)

Honeypot
14" • #5761 • HD
Issued: 1991 • Retired: 1994
Orig. Price: $27 • **Value: $150**

(7)

Hubbard W. Growler
12" • #5721-01 • AS
Issued: 1997 • Retired: 1998
Orig. Price: $21 • **Value: $38**

(8)

Huck
6" • #918051 • TJ
Issued: 1996 • Retired: 1998
Orig. Price: $12 • **Value: $23**

(9)

Humboldt
6" • #5840-05 • GB
Issued: 1996 • Current
Orig. Price: $9 • **Value: $9**

	Price Paid	Value Of My Collection
1.		
2.		
3.		
4.		
5.		
6.		
7.		
8.		
9.		

BEARS

PENCIL TOTALS

(1)

PHOTO UNAVAILABLE

Hume
info unavailable
Orig. Price: N/A • **Value: N/E**

(2)

Hurshel
12" • #5639-05 • BA
Issued: 1996 • Current
Orig. Price: $16 • **Value: $16**

(3)

Isaiah
10" • #917304 • TJ
Issued: 1996 • Retired: 1998
Orig. Price: $19 • **Value: $27**

(4)

J.B. Bean
10" • #5106 • JB
Issued: pre-1990 • Retired: 1997
Orig. Price: $14 • **Value: $33**

(5)

J.P. Huttin III
17" • #5110-08 • JB
Issued: 1995 • Retired: 1998
Orig. Price: $29 • **Value: $37**

(6)

Jackson R. Bearington
16" • #590021-05 • MB
Issued: 1998 • Retired: 1998
Orig. Price: $100 • **Value: $158**

BEARS

	Price Paid	Value Of My Collection
1.		
2.		
3.		
4.		
5.		
6.		
7.		
8.		
9.		
10.		

✎ PENCIL TOTALS

(7)

New!

Jameson J. Bearsford
6" • #57251-10 • AS
Issued: 1999 • Current
Orig. Price: $8 • **Value: $8**

(8)

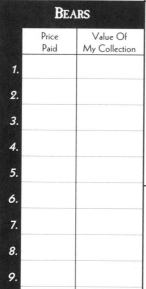

Jed Bruin
14" • #5123W • JB
Issued: 1992 • Retired: 1992
Orig. Price: $20 • **Value: $95**

(9)

Jefferson
8" • #1050-02 • DB
Issued: 1995 • Retired: 1996
Orig. Price: $11 • **Value: $48**

(10)

Jesse
11" • #1100-05 • CC
Issued: 1993 • Retired: 1995
Orig. Price: $10 • **Value: $50**

BEARS

1

Jethro
9" • #5630 • BA
Issued: 1995 • Retired: 1997
Orig. Price: $10 • **Value: $30**

2

Jody
16" • #5641-09 • BA
Issued: 1995 • Retired: 1996
Orig. Price: $24 • **Value: $42**

3

John
13" • #5828 • CB
Issued: 1992 • Retired: 1997
Orig. Price: $20 • **Value: $38**

4

Joshua
9" • #5826 • CB
Issued: 1992 • Retired: 1997
Orig. Price: $14 • **Value: $29**

5

New!

Katie B. Berrijam
10" • #910062 • TJ
Issued: 1999 • Current
Orig. Price: $23 • **Value: $23**

6

Katy Bear
info unavailable
Orig. Price: N/A • **Value: N/E**

7

Kip
8" • #5642-08 • BA
Issued: 1993 • Retired: 1997
Orig. Price: $11 • **Value: $29**

8

Klaus Von Fuzzner
14" • #91262 • TJ
Issued: 1998 • Current
Orig. Price: $40 • **Value: $40**

9

Knut V. Berriman
8" • #91231 • TJ
Issued: 1997 • Current
Orig. Price: $24 • **Value: $24**

10

Kringle Bear
10" • #9163 • TJ
Issued: 1993 • Retired: 1996
Orig. Price: $19 • **Value: $43**

BEARS		
	Price Paid	Value Of My Collection
1.		
2.		
3.		
4.		
5.		
6.		
7.		
8.		
9.		
10.		

✏ PENCIL TOTALS

1

Kringle Bear
14" • #9191 • TJ
Issued: 1993 • Retired: 1996
Orig. Price: $27 • **Value: $62**

2

Lacy
10" • #6100B • TJ
Issued: pre-1990 • Retired: 1992
Orig. Price: $16 • **Value: $110**

3

Lacy
10" • #6100DB • TJ
Issued: pre-1990 • Retired: 1991
Orig. Price: N/A • **Value: $110**

4

Lacy
14" • #6101B • TJ
Issued: pre-1990 • Retired: 1992
Orig. Price: $21 • **Value: $120**

5

Lacy
14" • #6101DB • TJ
Issued: pre-1990 • Retired: 1991
Orig. Price: N/A • **Value: $125**

6

Lancaster
8" • #57051-08 • AS
Issued: 1998 • Current
Orig. Price: $13 • **Value: $13**

BEARS

	Price Paid	Value Of My Collection
1.		
2.		
3.		
4.		
5.		
6.		
7.		
8.		
9.		

✎ **PENCIL TOTALS**

7

Lancelot
21" • #5722-11 • AS
Issued: 1996 • Current
Orig. Price: $53 • **Value: $53**

8

Lars
8" • #91735 • TJ
Issued: 1996 • Retired: 1997
Orig. Price: $18 • **Value: $32**

9

New!

Laurel S. Berrijam
6" • #913954 • TJ
Issued: 1999 • Current
Orig. Price: $13 • **Value: $13**

BEARS

1

Lem Bruin
14" • #5123 • JB
Issued: pre-1990 • Retired: 1993
Orig. Price: $20 • **Value: $75**

2

Leo Bruinski
10" • #918320 • TJ
Issued: 1998 • Current
Orig. Price: $31 • **Value: $31**

3

Leon
8" • #1001-08 • CC
Issued: 1993 • To Be Retired: 1999
Orig. Price: $6 • **Value: $7**

4

Lillian K. Bearsley
10" • #91743 • TJ
Issued: 1998 • Current
Orig. Price: $20 • **Value: $20**

5
New!

Lincoln B. Bearington
16" • #590022-08 • MB
Issued: 1999 • To Be Retired: 1999
Orig. Price: $100 • **Value: $100**

6

Linkin
6" • #5811 • SB
Issued: 1992 • Retired: 1995
Orig. Price: $7 • **Value: $45**

7

Lisa T. Bearringer
16" • #911950 • TJ
Issued: 1998 • Current
Orig. Price: $58 • **Value: $58**

8
New!

Liza J. Berrijam
10" • #910061 • TJ
Issued: 1999 • Current
Orig. Price: $17 • **Value: $17**

9

Lizzie McBee
8" • #91005 • TJ
Issued: 1996 • Retired: 1997
Orig. Price: $20 • **Value: $36**

10

Lloyd
10" • #5714 • AS
Issued: 1991 • Retired: 1992
Orig. Price: $18 • **Value: $135**

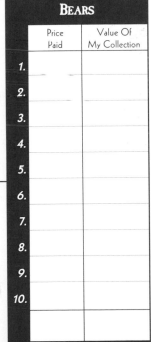

BEARS

	Price Paid	Value Of My Collection
1.		
2.		
3.		
4.		
5.		
6.		
7.		
8.		
9.		
10.		

✎ **PENCIL TOTALS**

(1)

Lou Bearig
6" • #91771-06 • TJ
Issued: 1998 • Current
Orig. Price: $14 • **Value: $14**

(2)

Louella
10" • #91242 • TJ
Issued: 1996 • Retired: 1998
Orig. Price: $24 • **Value: $32**

(3)

Louie B. Bear
16" • #5114-11 • JB
Issued: 1995 • Retired: 1997
Orig. Price: $27 • **Value: $44**

(4)

Lydia Fitzbruin
14" • #9182 • TJ
Issued: 1993 • Retired: 1996
Orig. Price: $27 • **Value: $75**

(5)

MacMillan
8" • #5705-10 • AS
Issued: 1995 • Retired: 1997
Orig. Price: $13 • **Value: $23**

(6)

Madison L. Bearington
6" • #590080-08 • MB
Issued: 1997 • Retired: 1997
Orig. Price: $18 • **Value: $30**

BEARS

	Price Paid	Value Of My Collection
1.		
2.		
3.		
4.		
5.		
6.		
7.		
8.		
9.		

(7)

Major
10" • #5717 • AS
Issued: 1991 • Retired: 1992
Orig. Price: $18 • **Value: $90**

(8)

Major II
10" • #5703B • AS
Issued: 1992 • Retired: 1995
Orig. Price: $18 • **Value: $40**

(9)

Malcolm
16" • #5711 • AS
Issued: 1992 • Current
Orig. Price: $32 • **Value: $32**

✏ PENCIL TOTALS

(1)

Margarita
14" • #911062 • TJ
Issued: 1998 • Current
Orig. Price: $20 • **Value: $20**

(2)
New!

Marlowe Snoopstein
11" • #91871 • TJ
Issued: 1999 • Current
Orig. Price: $23 • **Value: $23**

(3)

Marvin P. Snowbeary
6" • #9136-01 • TJ
Issued: 1997 • Current
Orig. Price: $12 • **Value: $12**

(4)

Matilda
N/A • #6161B • TJ
Issued: 1991 • Retired: 1991
Orig. Price: $63 • **Value: N/E**

(5)

Matthew (Fall 1996)
8" • #91756 • TJ
Issued: 1996 • Retired: 1997
Orig. Price: $26 • **Value: $40**

(6)

Matthew (Fall 1997)
8" • #91756-08 • TJ
Issued: 1997 • Retired: 1998
Orig. Price: $26 • **Value: $33**

(7)

Matthew (Fall 1998)
8" • #91756-10 • TJ
Issued: 1998 • To Be Retired: 1999
Orig. Price: $27 • **Value: $27**

(8)
PHOTO
UNAVAILABLE
Matthew Bear
10" • #5070 • N/A
Issued: N/A • Retired: N/A
Orig. Price: N/A • **Value: N/E**

(9)

Matthew H. Growler
12" • #5721 • AS
Issued: 1996 • To Be Retired: 1999
Orig. Price: $21 • **Value: $21**

(10)

McKenzie
6" • #5840-03 • GB
Issued: 1997 • Current
Orig. Price: $9 • **Value: $9**

	Price Paid	Value Of My Collection
BEARS		
1.		
2.		
3.		
4.		
5.		
6.		
7.		
8.		
9.		
10.		
PENCIL TOTALS		

McKinley
12" • #5848-05 • GB
Issued: 1996 • Current
Orig. Price: $21 • **Value: $21**

McMullen
12" • #5702 • AS
Issued: 1990 • Retired: 1991
Orig. Price: $20 • **Value: $100**

McShamus O'Growler
9" • #91732 • TJ
Issued: 1997 • Retired: 1998
Orig. Price: $21 • **Value: $36**

Melbourne
12" • #5719 • AS
Issued: 1992 • Retired: 1994
Orig. Price: $20 • **Value: $75**

Memsy
12" • N/A • N/A
Issued: N/A • Retired: N/A
Orig. Price: N/A • **Value: $385**

Mercedes Fitzbruin
8" • #91204 • TJ
Issued: 1998 • Current
Orig. Price: $19 • **Value: $19**

BEARS

	Price Paid	Value Of My Collection
1.		
2.		
3.		
4.		
5.		
6.		
7.		
8.		
9.		
10.		

PENCIL TOTALS

PHOTO UNAVAILABLE

Merlin
N/A • #6167B • TJ
Issued: 1991 • Retired: 1991
Orig. Price: $63 • **Value: N/E**

PHOTO UNAVAILABLE

Mickey
8" • #9157-01 • TJ
Issued: 1993 • Retired: 1994
Orig. Price: $14 • **Value: $60**

Milo
9" • #5767 • HD
Issued: 1992 • Retired: 1994
Orig. Price: $14 • **Value: $80**

New!

Minnie Higgenthorpe
6" • #918441 • TJ
Issued: 1999 • Current
Orig. Price: $10 • **Value: $10**

(1)

Miss Ashley
info unavailable
Orig. Price: N/A • **Value: N/E**

(2)

Missy
8" • #5642-10 • BA
Issued: 1995 • Retired: 1996
Orig. Price: $11 • **Value: $34**

(3)

Mistle
8.5" • #5151-04 • JB
Issued: 1994 • Retired: 1997
Orig. Price: $12 • **Value: $29**

(4)

Mohley
N/A • #5771 • HD
Issued: 1992 • Retired: 1992
Orig. Price: N/A • **Value: $120**

(5)

Momma McBear And Delmar
10" & 6" • #91007 • TJ
Issued: 1997 • Current
Orig. Price: $25 • **Value: $25**

(6)

Moriarity
11" • #9171 • TJ
Issued: 1993 • Retired: 1995
Orig. Price: $21 • **Value: $78**

(7)

Morris
8" • #1003-05 • CC
Issued: 1997 • Current
Orig. Price: $7 • **Value: $7**

(8)

Mr. Jones
16" • #5869-08 • AR
Issued: 1997 • Retired: 1998
Orig. Price: $37 • **Value: $45**

(9)

Mr. Smythe
12" • #58691-05 • AR
Issued: 1998 • Retired: 1998
Orig. Price: $27 • **Value: $35**

BEARS		
	Price Paid	Value Of My Collection
1.		
2.		
3.		
4.		
5.		
6.		
7.		
8.		
9.		
✎ PENCIL TOTALS		

(1)

Mr. Trumbull
10" • #918330 • TJ
Issued: 1998 • Current
Orig. Price: $28 • **Value: $28**

(2)

PHOTO UNAVAILABLE

Mrs. Bearberry
info unavailable
Orig. Price: N/A • **Value: $375**

(3)

PHOTO UNAVAILABLE

Mrs. Bearburg
info unavailable
Orig. Price: N/A • **Value: N/E**

(4)

PHOTO UNAVAILABLE

Mrs. Fiedler
info unavailable
Orig. Price: N/A • **Value: N/E**

(5)

New!

Mrs. Mertz
10" • #918331 • TJ
Issued: 1999 • Current
Orig. Price: $30 • **Value: $30**

(6)

Mrs. Trumbull
10" • #91833 • TJ
Issued: 1998 • Current
Orig. Price: $30 • **Value: $30**

BEARS

	Price Paid	Value Of My Collection
1.		
2.		
3.		
4.		
5.		
6.		
7.		
8.		
9.		
10.		

PENCIL TOTALS

(7)

Muffin
8" • #56421-03 • BA
Issued: 1998 • Current
Orig. Price: $11 • **Value: $11**

(8)

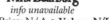

Nana
14" • #5765 • HD
Issued: 1991 • Retired: 1992
Orig. Price: $27 • **Value: $420**

(9)

Nanny Bear
info unavailable
Orig. Price: N/A • **Value: N/E**

(10)

Natasha Berriman
6" • #918050 • TJ
Issued: 1998 • Current
Orig. Price: $12 • **Value: $12**

BEARS

① Nellie

14" • #91105 • TJ
Issued: 1995 • Retired: 1997
Orig. Price: $20 • **Value: $44**

② Nelson

16" • #91261 • TJ
Issued: 1997 • Current
Orig. Price: $45 • **Value: $45**

③ Neville

5.5" • #5707 • AS
Issued: 1990 • Current
Orig. Price: $7 • **Value: $7**

④ Newton

8" • #9133 • TJ
Issued: 1994 • Retired: 1996
Orig. Price: $25 • **Value: $50**

⑤ Nicholas

8" • #9173 • TJ
Issued: 1993 • Retired: 1997
Orig. Price: $20 • **Value: $36**

⑥ Niki

6" • #91730 • TJ
Issued: 1996 • Retired: 1997
Orig. Price: $13 • **Value: $30**

⑦ Niki II

6" • #91730-1 • TJ
Issued: 1998 • Current
Orig. Price: $13 • **Value: $13**

⑧ Nod

6" • #5810 • SB
Issued: 1991 • Retired: 1992
Orig. Price: $7 • **Value: $47**

⑨ Nod II
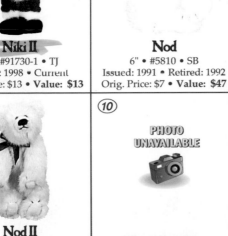
6" • #5810 • SB
Issued: 1992 • Current
Orig. Price: $7 • **Value: $7**

⑩ North Pole Bear

info unavailable
Orig. Price: N/A • **Value: N/E**

BEARS	Price Paid	Value Of My Collection
1		
2.		
3.		
4.		
5.		
6.		
7.		
8.		
9.		
10.		
✎ PENCIL TOTALS		

①

Ogden B. Bean
8" • #5153 • JB
Issued: 1994 • Current
Orig. Price: $12 • **Value: $13**

②

Olaf
12" • #9138 • TJ
Issued: 1994 • Retired: 1996
Orig. Price: $27 • **Value: $52**

③

Ophelia
16" • #91207-01 • TJ
Issued: 1997 • Retired: 1997
Orig. Price: $40 • **Value: $55**

④

Ophelia W. Witebred
16" • #91207 • TJ
Issued: 1996 • Retired: 1998
Orig. Price: $40 • **Value: $47**

⑤

Orville Bearington
4.5" • #590085-03 • MB
Issued: 1998 • Current
Orig. Price: $10 • **Value: $10**

⑥

Otis B. Bean
14" • #5107 • JB
Issued: pre-1990 • Retired: 1997
Orig. Price: $20 • **Value: $48**

BEARS

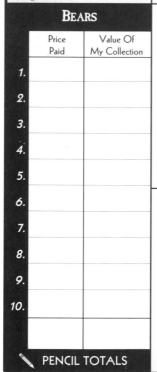

	Price Paid	Value Of My Collection
1.		
2.		
3.		
4.		
5.		
6.		
7.		
8.		
9.		
10.		

PENCIL TOTALS

⑦

Otto Von Bruin
6" • #5010 • WB
Issued: 1992 • Retired: 1994
Orig. Price: $9 • **Value: $41**

⑧ New!

Oxford T. Bearrister
12" • #57001-05 • AS
Issued: 1999 • Current
Orig. Price: $20 • **Value: $20**

⑨

Paddy McDoodle
9" • #51710 • BY
Issued: 1998 • Current
Orig. Price: $8 • **Value: $8**

⑩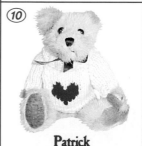

Patrick
8" • #9901 • TJ
Issued: 1995 • Retired: 1995
Orig. Price: $18 • **Value: $57**

①

Patsy
10" • #9100 • TJ
Issued: 1995 • Retired: 1996
Orig. Price: $20 • **Value: $54**

②

Paxton P. Bean
10" • #510300-05 • JB
Issued: 1998 • Current
Orig. Price: $14 • **Value: $14**

③

Peary
16" • #5807-10 • SB
Issued: 1998 • Current
Orig. Price: $29 • **Value: $29**

④

Pendleton J. Bruin
16" • #510400-11 • JB
Issued: 1998 • Current
Orig. Price: $27 • **Value: $26**

⑤

Perceval
10" • #5703-08 • AS
Issued: 1992 • To Be Retired: 1999
Orig. Price: $18 • **Value: $18**

⑥

Percy
5.5" • #5725-11 • AS
Issued: 1994 • Current
Orig. Price: $7 • **Value: $7**

⑦ New!

Perriwinkle P. Snicklefritz (musical)
8" • #51760-06 • BY
Issued: 1999 • Current
Orig. Price: $12 • **Value: $12**

⑧

Perry
8" • #1000-11 • CC
Issued: 1994 • Retired: 1997
Orig. Price: $6 • **Value: $29**

⑨

Phillip Bear Hop
11" • #9189 • TJ
Issued: 1991 • Retired: 1992
Orig. Price: $27 • **Value: $330**

⑩

Philomena
14" • #91106 • TJ
Issued: 1995 • Retired: 1997
Orig. Price: $20 • **Value: $44**

BEARS

	Price Paid	Value Of My Collection
1.		
2.		
3.		
4.		
5.		
6.		
7.		
8.		
9.		
10.		

✏ **PENCIL TOTALS**

1

PHOTO
UNAVAILABLE

Pinecone
info unavailable
Orig. Price: N/A • **Value: N/E**

2

Pohley
9" • #5768 • HD
Issued: 1991 • Retired: 1994
Orig. Price: $14 • **Value: $120**

3

Pop Bruin
16" • #5124 • JB
Issued: pre-1990 • Retired: 1995
Orig. Price: $27 • **Value: $68**

4

Poppa Bear & Noelle
10" & 5.5" • #917302 • JB
Issued: 1997 • Current
Orig. Price: $27 • **Value: $27**

5

New!

Prudence Bearimore
12" • #912053 • TJ
Issued: 1999 • Current
Orig. Price: $31 • **Value: $31**

6

Puck
8" • #9172 • TJ
Issued: 1993 • Retired: 1997
Orig. Price: $17 • **Value: $38**

BEARS

	Price Paid	Value Of My Collection
1.		
2.		
3.		
4.		
5.		
6.		
7.		
8.		
9.		

PENCIL TOTALS

7

New!

Quincy B. Bibbly
8.5" • #915611 • TJ
Issued: 1999 • Current
Orig. Price: $12 • **Value: $12**

8

Raleigh
10" • #5703M • AS
Issued: 1994 • Retired: 1997
Orig. Price: $18 • **Value: $34**

9

Reagan V. Bearington
8" • #590070-05 • MB
Issued: 1997 • Retired: 1997
Orig. Price: $24 • **Value: $50**

BEARS

1

Reva
9" • #5630-02 • BA
Issued: 1995 • Retired: 1997
Orig. Price: $10 • **Value: $26**

2

Rex
8" • #912440 • TJ
Issued: 1996 • Retired: 1998
Orig. Price: $18 • **Value: $25**

3

Rohley
9" • #5769 • HD
Issued: 1991 • Retired: 1992
Orig. Price: $14 • **Value: $160**

4

Roosevelt
14" • #6108B • JB
Issued: 1991 • Retired: 1992
Orig. Price: $27 • **Value: $225**

5

Roosevelt
8" • #9902 • TJ
Issued: 1995 • Retired: 1996
Orig. Price: $18 • **Value: $48**

6

Roosevelt P. Bearington
16" • #590020-08 • MB
Issued: 1997 • Retired: 1997
Orig. Price: $100 • **Value: $160**

7

Roxanne K. Bear
10" • #91741 • TJ
Issued: 1996 • Retired: 1998
Orig. Price: $20 • **Value: $25**

8

Royce
14" • #6107B • TJ
Issued: 1990 • Retired: 1992
Orig. Price: $32 • **Value: $265**

9

Rudolf
18" • #5807B • SB
Issued: 1992 • Retired: 1992
Orig. Price: N/A • **Value: $580**

10

Rufus Bear
16" • #5111 • JB
Issued: pre-1990 • Retired: 1998
Orig. Price: $27 • **Value: $44**

BEARS

	Price Paid	Value Of My Collection
1.		
2.		
3.		
4.		
5.		
6.		
7.		
8.		
9.		
10.		
PENCIL TOTALS		

①

Rupert
8" • #9142 • TJ
Issued: 1994 • Retired: 1996
Orig. Price: $18 • **Value: $53**

②

Rutherford
16" • #912610 • TJ
Issued: 1998 • Current
Orig. Price: $58 • **Value: $58**

③

S.C. Northstar
14" • #917303 • TJ
Issued: 1997 • Current
Orig. Price: $27 • **Value: $27**

④

St. Niklas
10" • #917311 • TJ
Issued: 1998 • Current
Orig. Price: $21 • **Value: $21**

⑤

Samuel
6" • #918052 • TJ
Issued: 1998 • Current
Orig. Price: $12 • **Value: $12**

⑥

Sandy Claus
16" • #91731 • TJ
Issued: 1995 • Retired: 1998
Orig. Price: $29 • **Value: $60**

BEARS

	Price Paid	Value Of My Collection
1.		
2.		
3.		
4.		
5.		
6.		
7.		
8.		
9.		
10.		

✏ PENCIL TOTALS

⑦

Sandy Claus II
16" • #917310 • TJ
Issued: 1998 • Current
Orig. Price: $29 • **Value: $29**

⑧

PHOTO UNAVAILABLE

Santa Bear
info unavailable
Orig. Price: N/A • **Value: N/E**

⑨

Sasha
10" • #9174 • TJ
Issued: 1995 • Retired: 1998
Orig. Price: $20 • **Value: $32**

⑩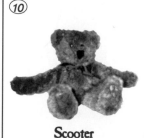

Scooter
8" • #5642-03 • BA
Issued: 1993 • Retired: 1995
Orig. Price: $11 • **Value: $50**

BEARS

①

Sebastian
13" • #5827 • CB
Issued: 1991 • Retired: 1997
Orig. Price: $20 • **Value: $42**

②

Seymour P. Snowbeary
12" • #9138-01 • TJ
Issued: 1997 • Current
Orig. Price: $27 • **Value: $27**

③

Sheldon Bearchild
6" • #918061 • TJ
Issued: 1998 • Current
Orig. Price: $8 • **Value: $8**

④

Sherlock
11" • #5821 • TJ
Issued: 1992 • Retired: 1992
Orig. Price: $20 • **Value: $110**

⑤

Sherlock
11" • #9188 • TJ
Issued: 1993 • Retired: 1997
Orig. Price: $21 • **Value: $40**

⑥

Sigmund Von Bruin
6" • #5010-08 • WB
Issued: 1994 • Retired: 1995
Orig. Price: $10 • **Value: $55**

⑦

Simone de Bearvoir
6" • #9180 • TJ
Issued: 1993 • Retired: 1996
Orig. Price: $9 • **Value: $35**

⑧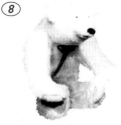

Sinkin
18" • #5808 • SB
Issued: 1991 • Retired: 1992
Orig. Price: $32 • **Value: $87**

⑨

Sinkin II
18" • #5808 • SB
Issued: 1992 • Retired: 1997
Orig. Price: $32 • **Value: $44**

⑩

Sir Henry
12" • #5720 • AS
Issued: 1991 • Retired: 1992
Orig. Price: $20 • **Value: $110**

BEARS

	Price Paid	Value Of My Collection
1.		
2.		
3.		
4.		
5.		
6.		
7.		
8.		
9.		
10.		

PENCIL TOTALS

(1)

Skidoo
11" • #9193 • TJ
Issued: 1992 • Retired: 1998
Orig. Price: $24 • **Value: $34**

(2)

Skip
12" • #5638 • BA
Issued: 1992 • Retired: 1996
Orig. Price: $16 • **Value: $40**

(3) New!

Skylar Thistlebeary
16" • #911951 • TJ
Issued: 1999 • Current
Orig. Price: $45 • **Value: $45**

(4)

Slugger
8" • #9177-01 • TJ
Issued: 1996 • To Be Retired: 1999
Orig. Price: $26 • **Value: $26**

(5)

Smith Witter II
17" • #5110 • JB
Issued: 1994 • Retired: 1998
Orig. Price: $29 • **Value: $40**

(6)

Sniffles
9" • #5773 • HD
Issued: 1991 • Retired: 1992
Orig. Price: $14 • **Value: $138**

BEARS

	Price Paid	Value Of My Collection
1.		
2.		
3.		
4.		
5.		
6.		
7.		
8.		
9.		

PENCIL TOTALS

(7)

Snowball
14" • #5123W • JB
Issued: 1992 • Retired: 1993
Orig. Price: N/A • **Value: $95**

(8)

Spencer
5.5" • #5725 • AS
Issued: 1993 • Current
Orig. Price: $7 • **Value: $7**

(9)

Squeeky
8" • #5615 • SQ
Issued: 1991 • Retired: 1991
Orig. Price: $10 • **Value: $105**

BEARS

1

Squeeky
8" • #5616 • SQ
Issued: 1992 • Retired: 1992
Orig. Price: $10 • **Value: $100**

2

PHOTO UNAVAILABLE

Stella Seamstress
info unavailable
Orig. Price: N/A • **Value: N/E**

3

New!

Stevenson Q. Bearitage
10" • #91736 • TJ
Issued: 1999 • Current
Orig. Price: $24 • **Value: $24**

4

PHOTO UNAVAILABLE

Stilton
info unavailable
Orig. Price: N/A • **Value: N/E**

5

PHOTO UNAVAILABLE

Stonewall Bear
info unavailable
Orig. Price: N/A • **Value: N/E**

6

Sven
8" • #9122 • TJ
Issued: 1994 • Retired: 1996
Orig. Price: $18 • **Value: $45**

7

T. Farley Wuzzie
5" • #595100-11 • TF
Issued: 1998 • Current
Orig. Price: $9 • **Value: $9**

8

T. Frasier Wuzzie
5" • #595100-08 • TF
Issued: 1998 • Current
Orig. Price: $9 • **Value: $9**

9

T. Fulton Wuzzie
5" • #595100-06 • TF
Issued: 1998 • Current
Orig. Price: $9 • **Value: $9**

10

New!

Tatum F. Wuzzie
3" • #596001 • TF
Issued: 1999 • Current
Orig. Price: $8 • **Value: $8**

	BEARS	
	Price Paid	Value Of My Collection
1.		
2.		
3.		
4.		
5.		
6.		
7.		
8.		
9.		
10.		
	PENCIL TOTALS	

Ted
8" • #9156 • TJ
Issued: 1993 • Retired: 1996
Orig. Price: $16 • **Value: $50**

Teddy Beanberger
(formerly "Teddy Beanbauer")
16" • #9118 • TJ
Issued: 1995 • Retired: 1997
Orig. Price: $53 • **Value: $72**

Thatcher
5.5" • #5706 • AS
Issued: 1990 • Retired: 1997
Orig. Price: $7 • **Value: $33**

Thayer
8.5" • #91570 • TJ
Issued: 1997 • Current
Orig. Price: $18 • **Value: $18**

Theodore
7.5" • #9196 • TJ
Issued: 1992 • Retired: 1994
Orig. Price: $16 • **Value: $50**

Thinkin
6" • #5809 • SB
Issued: 1991 • Retired: 1994
Orig. Price: $7 • **Value: $58**

BEARS

	Price Paid	Value Of My Collection
1.		
2.		
3.		
4.		
5.		
6.		
7.		
8.		
9.		
10.		

PENCIL TOTALS

New!

Thisbey F. Wuzzie
2.5" • #595160-02 • TF
Issued: 1999 • Current
Orig. Price: $7 • **Value: $7**

Thor M. Berriman
12" • #91734 • TJ
Issued: 1998 • Retired: 1998
Orig. Price: $30 • **Value: $42**

New!

Tilly F. Wuzzie
3" • #596000 • TF
Issued: 1999 • Current
Orig. Price: $8 • **Value: $8**

Timothy F. Wuzzie
3.5" • #595140 • TF
Issued: 1998 • Current
Orig. Price: $8 • **Value: $8**

①

Tinkin
10" • #5801 • SB
Issued: 1991 • Retired: 1992
Orig. Price: $20 • **Value: $70**

②

Tinkin II
10" • #5801 • SB
Issued: 1992 • Retired: 1997
Orig. Price: $20 • **Value: $42**

③

Toe
8.5" • #5151-02 • JB
Issued: 1994 • Retired: 1997
Orig. Price: $12 • **Value: $38**

④ New!

Tootie F. Wuzzie
2.5" • #595160-01 • TF
Issued: 1999 • Current
Orig. Price: $7 • **Value: $7**

⑤ New!

Townsend Q. Bearrister
12" • #57001-03 • AS
Issued: 1999 • Current
Orig. Price: $20 • **Value: $20**

⑥

Travis B. Bean
16" • #5114-05 • JB
Issued: 1993 • Retired: 1998
Orig. Price: $27 • **Value: $45**

⑦

PHOTO
UNAVAILABLE

Travis Bear
info unavailable
Orig. Price: N/A • **Value: N/E**

⑧

Tremont
16" • #56411-08 • BA
Issued: 1997 • Current
Orig. Price: $26 • **Value: $26**

⑨

Trevor F. Wuzzie
2.5" • #595160-08 • TF
Issued: 1997 • Current
Orig. Price: $7 • **Value: $7**

⑩

Truman S. Bearington
18" • #590010-05 • MB
Issued: 1998 • Retired: 1998
Orig. Price: $126 • **Value: $145**

BEARS

	Price Paid	Value Of My Collection
1.		
2.		
3.		
4.		
5.		
6.		
7.		
8.		
9.		
10.		
	PENCIL TOTALS	

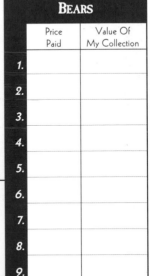

①

Tutu
N/A • #6169B • TJ
Issued: 1991 • Retired: 1991
Orig. Price: $63 • **Value: N/E**

②

Twila Higgenthorpe
6" • #91843 • TJ
Issued: 1997 • Current
Orig. Price: $10 • **Value: $10**

③
New!

Twilight F. Wuzzie
2.5" • #595160-06 • TF
Issued: 1999 • Current
Orig. Price: $7 • **Value: $7**

④

Twizzle F. Wuzzie
3.5" • #595141 • TF
Issued: 1998 • Current
Orig. Price: $8 • **Value: $8**

⑤

Tylar F. Wuzzie
2.5" • #595160-11 • TF
Issued: 1997 • Current
Orig. Price: $7 • **Value: $7**

⑥

Tyler Summerfield
12" • #9124 • TJ
Issued: 1996 • Retired: 1997
Orig. Price: $37 • **Value: $55**

BEARS

	Price Paid	Value Of My Collection
1.		
2.		
3.		
4.		
5.		
6.		
7.		
8.		
9.		
10.		

✏ PENCIL TOTALS

⑦

Tyrone F. Wuzzie
2.5" • #595160-05 • TF
Issued: 1997 • Current
Orig. Price: $7 • **Value: $7**

⑧

Ursa
14" • #5720-07 • AS
Issued: 1995 • Retired: 1998
Orig. Price: $24 • **Value: $35**

⑨

Varsity Bear
info unavailable
Orig. Price: N/A • **Value: $140**

⑩

Varsity Bear
N/A • #9198 • N/A
Issued: 1992 • Retired: 1992
Orig. Price: N/A • **Value: $250**

BEARS

①

Vincent
11" • #1100-11 • CC
Issued: 1995 • Retired: 1997
Orig. Price: $10 • **Value: $26**

②

Walpole
8" • #5705M • AS
Issued: 1993 • Retired: 1997
Orig. Price: $13 • **Value: $29**

③

Walton
11" • #9128 • TJ
Issued: 1994 • Retired: 1997
Orig. Price: $21 • **Value: $38**

④

Warren
8" • #1002-01 • CC
Issued: 1993 • Retired: 1997
Orig. Price: $6 • **Value: $32**

⑤
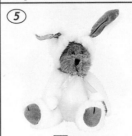
Watson
8" • #9187 • TJ
Issued: 1993 • To Be Retired: 1999
Orig. Price: $17 • **Value: $17**

⑥

Wellington
21" • #5722 • AS
Issued: 1992 • Retired: 1997
Orig. Price: $53 • **Value: $70**

⑦

Werner Von Bruin
6" • #5010-11 • WB
Issued: 1993 • Retired: 1995
Orig. Price: $10 • **Value: $46**

⑧

Wheaton Flatski
8" • #5680-10 • FL
Issued: 1996 • Retired: 1996
Orig. Price: $13 • **Value: $52**

⑨

Whitaker Q. Bruin
5.5" • #91806 • TJ
Issued: 1996 • Retired: 1998
Orig. Price: $11 • **Value: $15**

⑩
PHOTO
UNAVAILABLE
White Bean Bear
info unavailable
Orig. Price: N/A • **Value: N/E**

	Price Paid	Value Of My Collection
1.		
2.		
3.		
4.		
5.		
6.		
7.		
8.		
9.		
10.		

BEARS

✏ PENCIL TOTALS

(1)

Wilbur Bearington
4.5" • #590085-10 • MB
Issued: 1998 • Current
Orig. Price: $10 • **Value: $10**

(2)

New!

Wilcox J. Beansford
14" • #51081-05 • JB
Issued: 1999 • Current
Orig. Price: $20 • **Value: $20**

(3)

Willa Bruin
11" • #91205 • TJ
Issued: 1995 • Retired: 1997
Orig. Price: $30 • **Value: $43**

(4)

William P.
12" • #1107-03 • CC
Issued: 1998 • Current
Orig. Price: $12 • **Value: $12**

(5)

Willmar Flatski
8" • #56801-05 • FL
Issued: 1998 • Current
Orig. Price: $13 • **Value: $13**

(6)

Wilson
8" • #5705 • AS
Issued: 1990 • Retired: 1997
Orig. Price: $12 • **Value: $30**

BEARS

	Price Paid	Value Of My Collection
1.		
2.		
3.		
4.		
5.		
6.		
7.		
8.		
9.		
10.		

✏ PENCIL TOTALS

(7)

Winifred Witebred
14" • #912071 • TJ
Issued: 1998 • Current
Orig. Price: $34 • **Value: $34**

(8)

Winkie II
12" • #5639-08 • BA
Issued: 1992 • Retired: 1998
Orig. Price: $16 • **Value: $20**

(9)

Winkin
10" • #5800 • SB
Issued: 1991 • Retired: 1993
Orig. Price: $20 • **Value: $70**

(10)

Winnie II
14" • #912071-01 • TJ
Issued: 1998 • Current
Orig. Price: $34 • **Value: $34**

BEARS

① New!

Winnie Wuzzwhite
14" • #912071-02 • TJ
Issued: 1999 • Current
Orig. Price: $34 • **Value: $34**

②

Winstead P. Bear
15" • #515210-03 • JB
Issued: 1998 • Current
Orig. Price: $24 • **Value: $24**

③

Winston B. Bean
10" • #5104 • JB
Issued: pre-1990 • Retired: 1996
Orig. Price: $14 • **Value: $35**

④

Witch-A-Ma-Call-It
info unavailable
Orig. Price: N/A • **Value: N/E**

⑤ New!

Woodrow T. Bearington
12" • #590041-03 • MB
Issued: 1999 • To Be Retired: 1999
Orig. Price: $48 • **Value: $48**

⑥

Worthington Fitzbruin
8.5" • #912032 • TJ
Issued: 1997 • Current
Orig. Price: $14 • **Value: $14**

⑦ New!

Yardley Fitzhampton
14" • #912030 • TJ
Issued: 1999 • Current
Orig. Price: $27 • **Value: $27**

⑧

Yogi
6" • #91771-02 • TJ
Issued: 1997 • Current
Orig. Price: $14 • **Value: $14**

⑨

Yolanda Panda
6" • #57701 • AS
Issued: 1998 • Current
Orig. Price: $9 • **Value: $9**

⑩

York
8" • #57051-05 • AS
Issued: 1998 • Current
Orig. Price: $13 • **Value: $13**

BEARS		
	Price Paid	Value Of My Collection
1.		
2.		
3.		
4.		
5.		
6.		
7.		
8.		
9.		
10.		
	PENCIL TOTALS	

①

Yvette DuBeary
6" • #918431 • TJ
Issued: 1999 • Current
Orig. Price: $10 • **Value: $10**

②

Zazu
16" • #5641-05 • BA
Issued: 1996 • Current
Orig. Price: $26 • **Value: $26**

③

Ziggy Bear
12" • #5060 • N/A
Issued: N/A • Retired: N/A
Orig. Price: N/A • **Value: N/E**

CATS

Every year since their debut, there has been a new litter of kittens in the Boyds family. This year, eight new cats join the group, while five will be honored with retirement status in 1999. This branch of the family tree, which includes the popular Grimilkins and Catbergs, is made up of 74 characters.

④

Allie Fuzzbucket
9" • #51720 • BY
Issued: 1998 • Current
Orig. Price: $8 • **Value: $8**

BEARS

	Price Paid	Value Of My Collection
1.		
2.		
3.		

CATS

4.		
5.		
6.		
7.		
8.		

✏ PENCIL TOTALS

⑤

Baby
11" • #6105C • TJ
Issued: 1990 • Retired: 1990
Orig. Price: N/A • **Value: $280**

⑥
New!

Boots Alleyruckus
14" • #5308-07 • JB
Issued: 1999 • Current
Orig. Price: $20 • **Value: $20**

⑦

Bronte
5.5" • #5742-10 • AS
Issued: 1994 • Retired: 1996
Orig. Price: $8 • **Value: $46**

⑧

Browning
8" • #5741 • AS
Issued: 1992 • To Be Retired: 1999
Orig. Price: $12 • **Value: $12**

CATS

① Byron

8" • #5740 • AS
Issued: 1992 • To Be Retired: 1999
Orig. Price: $12 • **Value: $12**

② Cabin Cat

PHOTO UNAVAILABLE
info unavailable
Orig. Price: N/A • **Value: N/E**

③ Callaway Flatcat

8" • #56951-06 • FL
Issued: 1998 • Current
Orig. Price: $13 • **Value: $13**

④ Candy Corn Cat

8" • #91971 • TJ
Issued: 1995 • Retired: 1997
Orig. Price: $18 • **Value: $43**

⑤ Catherine Q. Fuzzberg

8" • #5303-08 • JB
Issued: 1997 • Current
Orig. Price: $10 • **Value: $10**

⑥ Chaucer
8" • #9135 • TJ
Issued: 1994 • Retired: 1995
Orig. Price: $20 • **Value: $49**

⑦ Chaucer

8" • #9135-01 • TJ
Issued: 1994 • Retired: 1995
Orig. Price: $20 • **Value: $46**

⑧ Claudine de la Plumtete
New!

6" • #91710 • TJ
Issued: 1999 • Current
Orig. Price: $9 • **Value: $9**

⑨ Cleo P. Pussytoes

16" • #91209 • TJ
Issued: 1997 • Current
Orig. Price: $40 • **Value: $40**

⑩ Cookie Grimilkin

11" • #5306 • JB
Issued: 1991 • Current
Orig. Price: $14 • **Value: $14**

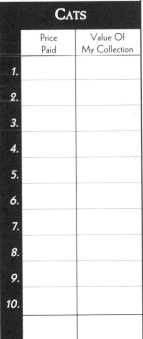

CATS

	Price Paid	Value Of My Collection
1.		
2.		
3.		
4.		
5.		
6.		
7.		
8.		
9.		
10.		
✎ PENCIL TOTALS		

(1)

Cuthbert Catberg
16" • #5314 • JB
Issued: 1992 • Retired: 1993
Orig. Price: N/A • **Value: $112**

(2)

Dewey Q. Grimilkin
info unavailable
Orig. Price: N/A • **Value: $117**

(3)

Dewey R. Cat
11" • #5302T • JB
Issued: 1990 • Retired: 1990
Orig. Price: N/A • **Value: $135**

(4)

PHOTO
UNAVAILABLE

Eleanor
info unavailable
Orig. Price: N/A • **Value: N/E**

(5)

Ellsworth Flatcat II
8" • #5695-08 • FL
Issued: 1994 • Current
Orig. Price: $12 • **Value: $13**

(6)

Ernest Q. Grimilkin
11" • #5304 • JB
Issued: pre-1990 • Current
Orig. Price: $14 • **Value: $14**

CATS

	Price Paid	Value Of My Collection
1.		
2.		
3.		
4.		
5.		
6.		
7.		
8.		
9.		
10.		

(7)

Felina B. Catterwall
8" • #919701 • TJ
Issued: 1998 • Current
Orig. Price: $12 • **Value: $12**

(8)

Fraid E. Cat
5.5" • #9198 • TJ
Issued: 1994 • Retired: 1997
Orig. Price: $12 • **Value: $34**

(9)

Gae Q. Grimilkin
14" • #5324 • JB
Issued: pre-1990 • Retired: 1992
Orig. Price: $20 • **Value: $135**

(10)

PHOTO
UNAVAILABLE

Gardner
info unavailable
Orig. Price: $63 • **Value: N/E**

✏ PENCIL TOTALS

(1)

Garner J. Cattington
10" • #590250-11 • MB
Issued: 1998 • Retired: 1998
Orig. Price: $31 • **Value: $45**

(2)

Glenwood Flatcat
8" • #56951-08 • FL
Issued: 1998 • Current
Orig. Price: $13 • **Value: $13**

(3)

PHOTO UNAVAILABLE

Grace
info unavailable
Orig. Price: $63 • **Value: N/E**

(4)

Greybeard
16" • #5312 • JB
Issued: 1991 • Retired: 1993
Orig. Price: $29 • **Value: $140**

(5)

Hattie
6" • #9105 • TJ
Issued: 1995 • Retired: 1997
Orig. Price: $12 • **Value: $30**

(6)

Heranamous
16" • #5311-07 • JB
Issued: 1996 • Current
Orig. Price: $29 • **Value: $29**

(7)

Holloway Flatcat
8" • #5695-07 • FL
Issued: 1994 • Current
Orig. Price: $12 • **Value: $13**

(8)

Inky Catterwall
8" • #91972 • TJ
Issued: 1998 • Current
Orig. Price: $18 • **Value: $18**

(9)

New!

Kattelina Purrsley
11" • #91978 • TJ
Issued: 1999 • Current
Orig. Price: $20 • **Value: $20**

(10)

Keats
5.5" • #5743 • AS
Issued: 1992 • Current
Orig. Price: $8 • **Value: $8**

CATS

	Price Paid	Value Of My Collection
1.		
2.		
3.		
4.		
5.		
6.		
7.		
8.		
9.		
10.		

PENCIL TOTALS

CATS

New!

Kitt Purrsley
8" • #91711 • TJ
Issued: 1999 • Current
Orig. Price: $18 • **Value: $18**

Lacy
10" • #6100C • TJ
Issued: 1990 • Retired: 1992
Orig. Price: $16 • **Value: $115**

Lacy
14" • #6101C • TJ
Issued: 1990 • Retired: 1991
Orig. Price: $21 • **Value: $92**

New!

Lindbergh Cattington
4.5" • #590087-03 • MB
Issued: 1999 • Current
Orig. Price: $10 • **Value: $10**

Lindsey P. Pussytoes
12" • #912091 • TJ
Issued: 1998 • Current
Orig. Price: $31 • **Value: $31**

New!

Lola Ninelives
9" • #919751 • TJ
Issued: 1999 • Current
Orig. Price: $24 • **Value: $24**

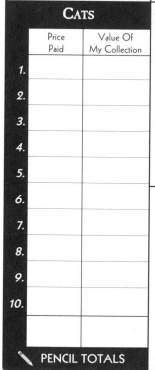

CATS

	Price Paid	Value Of My Collection
1.		
2.		
3.		
4.		
5.		
6.		
7.		
8.		
9.		
10.		

✎ PENCIL TOTALS

Millicent P. Pussytoes
11" • #91976 • TJ
Issued: 1997 • Retired: 1998
Orig. Price: $20 • **Value: $32**

Mrs. Partridge
9" • #919750 • TJ
Issued: 1998 • Current
Orig. Price: $30 • **Value: $30**

Ned
12" • #5656-03 • BA
Issued: 1993 • Retired: 1995
Orig. Price: $16 • **Value: $53**

Opel Catberg
14" • #5324-10 • JB
Issued: 1995 • To Be Retired: 1999
Orig. Price: $20 • **Value: $20**

(1)

Ophilia Q. Grimilkin
14" • #5323 • JB
Issued: pre-1990 • Retired: 1990
Orig. Price: $20 • **Value: $165**

(2)

Pearl Catberg
14" • #5324-01 • JB
Issued: 1994 • Retired: 1995
Orig. Price: $20 • **Value: $88**

(3)

Poe
5.5" • #5742-07 • AS
Issued: 1993 • Current
Orig. Price: $8 • **Value: $8**

(4)

Punkin Puss
8" • #9197 • TJ
Issued: 1992 • Retired: 1997
Orig. Price: $18 • **Value: $40**

(5)

Puss N. Boo
8" • #9164 • TJ
Issued: 1993 • Retired: 1995
Orig. Price: $18 • **Value: $52**

(6)

PHOTO UNAVAILABLE

Royce
info unavailable
Orig. Price: $32 • **Value: N/E**

(7)

Sabrina P. Catterwall
8" • #919700 • TJ
Issued: 1998 • Current
Orig. Price: $12 • **Value: $12**

(8)

PHOTO UNAVAILABLE

Samuel Catberg
info unavailable
Orig. Price: N/A • **Value: N/E**

(9)

Shelly
5.5" • #5742 • AS
Issued: 1992 • Current
Orig. Price: $8 • **Value: $8**

(10)

Socks Grimilkin
14" • #5324-07 • JB
Issued: 1993 • Retired: 1998
Orig. Price: $20 • **Value: $35**

CATS

	Price Paid	Value Of My Collection
1.		
2.		
3.		
4.		
5.		
6.		
7.		
8.		
9.		
10.		

✎ **PENCIL TOTALS**

CATS

(1) Spiro T. Cattington
12" • #590240-07 • MB
Issued: 1998 • Retired: 1998
Orig. Price: $51 • **Value: $68**

(2) Spooky Tangaween
11" • #91975 • TJ
Issued: 1996 • Retired: 1998
Orig. Price: $20 • **Value: $32**

(3) Suzie Purrkins
11" • #91977 • TJ
Issued: 1998 • Retired: 1998
Orig. Price: $20 • **Value: $29**

(4) Sweetpea Catberg
11" • #5305 • JB
Issued: pre-1990 • Retired: 1992
Orig. Price: $14 • **Value: $67**

(5) Sweetpea Catberg
11" • #5307 • JB
Issued: 1992 • Retired: 1998
Orig. Price: $14 • **Value: $25**

(6) New!

Tabby F. Wuzzie
3" • #595240-07 • TF
Issued: 1999 • Current
Orig. Price: $7 • **Value: $7**

CATS

	Price Paid	Value Of My Collection
1.		
2.		
3.		
4.		
5.		
6.		
7.		
8.		
9.		

PENCIL TOTALS

(7) Tennyson
5.5" • #5744 • AS
Issued: 1992 • Current
Orig. Price: $8 • **Value: $8**

(8) Thom
12" • #5656-07 • BA
Issued: 1993 • Retired: 1995
Orig. Price: $16 • **Value: $43**

(9) Thoreau
8" • #5740-08 • AS
Issued: 1995 • To Be Retired: 1999
Orig. Price: $12 • **Value: $12**

①

Tigerlily
16" • #5311 • JB
Issued: pre-1990 • Retired: 1995
Orig. Price: $29 • **Value: $40**

②
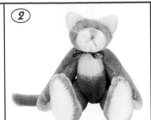
Turner F. Wuzzie
3" • #595240-06 • TF
Issued: 1998 • Current
Orig. Price: $7 • **Value: $7**

③

Walter Q. Fuzzberg
8" • #5303-07 • JB
Issued: 1997 • Current
Orig. Price: $10 • **Value: $10**

④
New!

Zachariah Alleyruckus
14" • #5308-06 • JB
Issued: 1999 • Current
Orig. Price: $20 • **Value: $20**

⑤

Zap Catberg
14" • #5325 • JB
Issued: 1992 • Retired: 1992
Orig. Price: $20 • **Value: N/E**

⑥

Zelda Catberg
14" • #5324-06 • JB
Issued: 1993 • Retired: 1993
Orig. Price: N/A • **Value: $79**

⑦

Zenus W. Grimilkin
11" • #5303 • JB
Issued: pre-1990 • Retired: 1991
Orig. Price: $14 • **Value: $155**

⑧

Zip Catberg
14" • #5325 • JB
Issued: pre-1990 • Retired: 1992
Orig. Price: $20 • **Value: $130**

⑨

Zoe R. Grimilkin
11" • #5304-07 • JB
Issued: 1994 • To Be Retired: 1999
Orig. Price: $14 • **Value: $14**

⑩

Zoom Catberg
14" • #5326 • JB
Issued: 1992 • Retired: 1993
Orig. Price: $20 • **Value: $135**

CATS

	Price Paid	Value Of My Collection
1.		
2.		
3.		
4.		
5.		
6.		
7.		
8.		
9.		
10.		

✎ PENCIL TOTALS

CATS

COWS

It will be a busy year on the farm in 1999 when three new cows join the herd, bringing the total available to 12. While there have been no retirements scheduled for 1999, seven bovine friends have already been sent to the pasture.

New!

Angus MacMoo
11" • #91341 • TJ
Issued: 1999 • Current
Orig. Price: $20 • **Value: $20**

Bertha Utterberg
8" • #5758 • AS
Issued: 1996 • Retired: 1996
Orig. Price: $13 • **Value: $45**

Bessie Moostein
11" • #5532 • AM
Issued: 1991 • Current
Orig. Price: $14 • **Value: $14**

Elmer Beefcake
14" • #5535-11 • AM
Issued: 1995 • Retired: 1996
Orig. Price: $20 • **Value: $54**

COWS

	Price Paid	Value Of My Collection
1.		
2.		
3.		
4.		
5.		
6.		
7.		
8.		

✎ PENCIL TOTALS

Elmo Beefcake
11" • #5532-03 • AM
Issued: 1993 • Retired: 1998
Orig. Price: $14 • **Value: $30**

New!

Ernestine Vanderhoof
8" • #55312-05 • AM
Issued: 1999 • Current
Orig. Price: $11 • **Value: $11**

Herman Beefcake
16" • #5534 • AM
Issued: 1992 • Retired: 1994
Orig. Price: $27 • **Value: $100**

Hester
12" • #5660-10 • BA
Issued: 1996 • Retired: 1997
Orig. Price: $16 • **Value: $28**

①

Hortense Moostein
16" • #5533 • AM
Issued: 1992 • Retired: 1995
Orig. Price: $29 • **Value: $80**

②

Ida Moostein
14" • #5535-10 • AM
Issued: 1994 • Retired: 1996
Orig. Price: $20 • **Value: $46**

③

Sadie Utterburg
16" • #5533-10 • AM
Issued: 1996 • Current
Orig. Price: $29 • **Value: $29**

④

New!

Silo Q. Vanderhoof
8" • #55312-07 • AM
Issued: 1999 • Current
Orig. Price: $11 • **Value: $11**

CROWS

The only birds to have ever been a part of the Boyds Collection, "Edgar" and "Hank Krow Jr." were both members of the *Artisan Series*. Both flew into retirement in 1997.

⑤

Edgar
6" • #5864-07 • AR
Issued: 1996 • Retired: 1997
Orig. Price: $9 • **Value: $39**

⑥

Hank Krow Jr.
11" • #5865-07 • AR
Issued: 1995 • Retired: 1997
Orig. Price: $14 • **Value: $33**

COWS/CROWS

	Price Paid	Value Of My Collection
COWS		
1.		
2.		
3.		
4.		
CROWS		
5.		
6.		

✎ PENCIL TOTALS

DOGS

"Speed Poochberg" and "Roosevelt" made their debut as the first Boyds canines to join the Boyds family. Since then, they have been joined by 23 others, including three new pooches in 1999.

Arno-w-ld
12" • #5655-07 • BA
Issued: 1996 • Retired: 1997
Orig. Price: $16 • **Value: $48**

Bagley Flatberg
8" • #5690-03 • FL
Issued: 1996 • Current
Orig. Price: $13 • **Value: $13**

New!

Barkley McFarkle
9" • #51750 • BY
Issued: 1999 • Current
Orig. Price: $8 • **Value: $8**

Betty Biscuit
10" • #5402-08 • JB
Issued: 1995 • Retired: 1997
Orig. Price: $14 • **Value: $32**

DOGS

	Price Paid	Value Of My Collection
1.		
2.		
3.		
4.		
5.		
6.		
7.		

PENCIL TOTALS

Beulah Canine
11" • #5403 • JB
Issued: pre-1990 • Retired: 1991
Orig. Price: $14 • **Value: N/E**

Clancy G. Hydrant, Jr.
10" • #5404 • JB
Issued: 1998 • Current
Orig. Price: $14 • **Value: $15**

Collier P. Hydrant II
16" • #5403 • JB
Issued: 1997 • Current
Orig. Price: $29 • **Value: $29**

①

Fritz Von Bruin
6" • #5014 • WB
Issued: 1992 • Retired: 1992
Orig. Price: N/A • **Value: $200**

②

Hector Flatberg
8" • #5690-07 • FL
Issued: 1995 • Retired: 1996
Orig. Price: $13 • **Value: $33**

③

Hercules Von Mutt
6" • #5014-01 • WB
Issued: 1993 • Retired: 1994
Orig. Price: $10 • **Value: $50**

④

Indy (Fall 1997)
5.5" • #91757 • TJ
Issued: 1997 • Retired: 1998
Orig. Price: $12 • **Value: $24**

⑤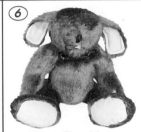

Indy (Fall 1998)
5.5" • #91757-10 • TJ
Issued: 1998 • To Be Retired: 1999
Orig. Price: $12 • **Value: $12**

⑥

Irving Poochberg
14" • #5420 • JB
Issued: pre-1990 • Retired: 1992
Orig. Price: $16 • **Value: $135**

⑦

Martin Muttski
11" • #5400 • JB
Issued: pre-1990 • Retired: 1992
Orig. Price: $14 • **Value: $115**

⑧

Merritt M. Mutt
11" • #5401 • JB
Issued: pre-1990 • Retired: 1991
Orig. Price: $14 • **Value: $115**

⑨

Merton Flatberg
8" • #5690-08 • FL
Issued: 1994 • Retired: 1997
Orig. Price: $12 • **Value: $27**

DOGS

	Price Paid	Value Of My Collection
1.		
2.		
3.		
4.		
5.		
6.		
7.		
8.		
9.		

✎ PENCIL TOTALS

DOGS

(1)

Northrop Flatberg
8" • #5690-01 • FL
Issued: 1994 • Current
Orig. Price: $12 • **Value: $13**

(2) New!

Philo Puddlemaker
12" • #56551-07 • BA
Issued: 1999 • Current
Orig. Price: $16 • **Value: $16**

(3)

Preston
12" • #56961-01 • FL
Issued: 1996 • Retired: 1996
Orig. Price: N/A • **Value: N/E**

(4)

Ralph Poochstein
10" • #5400-10 • JB
Issued: 1995 • Retired: 1997
Orig. Price: $14 • **Value: $34**

(5)

PHOTO UNAVAILABLE

Roosevelt
15" • #6108D • TJ
Issued: pre-1990 • Retired: 1991
Orig. Price: $27 • **Value: $150**

(6)

Speed Poochberg
11" • #5402 • JB
Issued: pre-1990 • Retired: 1992
Orig. Price: $14 • **Value: $120**

DOGS

	Price Paid	Value Of My Collection
1.		
2.		
3.		
4.		
5.		
6.		
7.		
8.		
9.		

✏ PENCIL TOTALS

(7) New!

Toby F. Wuzzie
3" • #595500-08 • TF
Issued: 1999 • Current
Orig. Price: $7 • **Value: $7**

(8)

Unidentified Dog
10" • N/A • N/A
Issued: N/A • Retired: N/A
Orig. Price: N/A • **Value: N/E**

(9)

Walker
12" • #5655-08 • BA
Issued: 1994 • Retired: 1997
Orig. Price: $16 • **Value: $33**

DONKEYS

Introduced in 1996, "Brayburn" is the only donkey to mosey into the general Boyds collection. Collectors who wished to add this long-eared lovely to their collection had to act fast as his political career was short-lived and "Brayburn" was retired in 1997.

Brayburn
8" • #5670 • FL
Issued: 1996 • Retired: 1997
Orig. Price: $13 • **Value: $37**

ELEPHANTS

In 1993, the Pachydermsky's moved into the Boyds neighborhood. Their stay was brief however, lasting only one year. Only one other elephant has been introduced into the general line since, and while known for their long memory, they're not known for long production runs as "Newton" was retired in 1997, also becoming just a memory for many collectors.

Newton
8" • #5665 • FL
Issued: 1996 • Retired: 1997
Orig. Price: $13 • **Value: $35**

Nicolai A. Pachydermsky
16" • #5528-06 • AM
Issued: 1993 • Retired: 1994
Orig. Price: $28 • **Value: $230**

Olivia A. Pachydermsky
10" • #5527-06 • AM
Issued: 1993 • Retired: 1994
Orig. Price: $14 • **Value: $120**

Omar A. Pachydermsky
7.5" • #5526-06 • AM
Issued: 1993 • Retired: 1994
Orig. Price: $8 • **Value: $92**

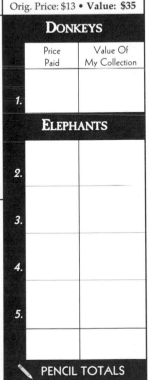

DONKEYS		
	Price Paid	Value Of My Collection
1.		
ELEPHANTS		
2.		
3.		
4.		
5.		
PENCIL TOTALS		

DONKEYS/ELEPHANTS

FROGS

"G. Kelly Ribbit" sings and dances his way into the line in 1999, bringing the total number of frogs to six. Four of these amphibious pals are still enjoying life on the pond, while two have been ordered "outta the pool" by the "Head Bean," including "Jeremiah B. Ribbit," who will be retired in 1999.

Ezra R. Ribbit
6" • #566470 • BA
Issued: 1998 • Current
Orig. Price: $5 • **Value: $5**

New!

G. Kelly Ribbit (musical)
9" • #91320 • TJ
Issued: 1999 • Current
Orig. Price: $25 • **Value: $25**

Jacque Le Grenouille
8" • #5018 • WB
Issued: 1993 • Retired: 1995
Orig. Price: $10 • **Value: $48**

Jeremiah B. Ribbit
9.5" • #566450 • BA
Issued: 1997 • To Be Retired: 1999
Orig. Price: $12 • **Value: $12**

FROGS

	Price Paid	Value Of My Collection
1.		
2.		
3.		
4.		
5.		
6.		

✎ PENCIL TOTALS

Racheal Q. Ribbit
12" • #566340 • BA
Issued: 1997 • Current
Orig. Price: $21 • **Value: $21**

S.C. Ribbit (musical)
12" • #917309 • TJ
Issued: 1998 • Current
Orig. Price: $25 • **Value: $25**

GORILLAS

The Boyds family of gorillas continues to grow in 1999 as "Viola Magillacuddy" becomes the first female gorilla to join the clan. While one of these pieces was honored with retirement in 1998, two of them are currently available.

Joe Magilla
11" • #5525 • AM
Issued: 1995 • Retired: 1998
Orig. Price: $14 • **Value: $26**

Mike Magilla
8" • #55251 • AM
Issued: 1998 • Current
Orig. Price: $12 • **Value: $12**

New!

Viola Magillacuddy
8" • #91351 • TJ
Issued: 1999 • Current
Orig. Price: $14 • **Value: $14**

HARES

Hares make up the second most populous of the Boyds categories. So far, 224 rabbits have hopped into the Boyds line since its inception, including 23 new pieces introduced in 1999. While new hare pieces continue to top off the line each season, they often retire quickly, with only 59 of the pieces holding current status, nine of which will retire in 1999.

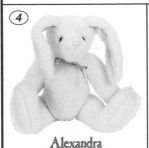

Alexandra
14" • #5730 • AS
Issued: 1991 • Retired: 1995
Orig. Price: $20 • **Value: $114**

Alice
7.5" • #5750 • AS
Issued: 1992 • Current
Orig. Price: $7 • **Value: $7**

GORILLAS		
	Price Paid	Value Of My Collection
1.		
2.		
3.		

HARES		
4.		
5.		
PENCIL TOTALS		

GORILLAS/HARES

① Allison Babbit
14" • #9166 • TJ
Issued: 1994 • Retired: 1998
Orig. Price: $20 • **Value: $26**

② Amarretto
17" • #9110 • TJ
Issued: 1995 • Retired: 1997
Orig. Price: $19 • **Value: $32**

③ Amelia R. Hare
12" • #5203 • JB
Issued: pre-1990 • Retired: 1998
Orig. Price: $14 • **Value: $24**

④

Anastasia
14" • #5876 • HT
Issued: 1992 • Retired: 1992
Orig. Price: $32 • **Value: $84**

⑤ Anastasia
12" • #912081 • TJ
Issued: 1998 • Current
Orig. Price: $26 • **Value: $26**

⑥ Anisette
12" • #9109-07 • TJ
Issued: 1996 • Retired: 1996
Orig. Price: $12 • **Value: $42**

HARES

	Price Paid	Value Of My Collection
1.		
2.		
3.		
4.		
5.		
6.		
7.		
8.		
9.		
10.		

 PENCIL TOTALS

⑦ Anna
6" • #5870 • HT
Issued: 1992 • Retired: 1993
Orig. Price: $9 • **Value: $88**

⑧ Anne
7.5" • #5734 • AS
Issued: 1991 • Retired: 1997
Orig. Price: $7 • **Value: $23**

⑨ Archer
10" • #91544 • TJ
Issued: 1996 • Retired: 1998
Orig. Price: $24 • **Value: $38**

⑩ Ashley
12" • #9132 • TJ
Issued: 1995 • Retired: 1998
Orig. Price: $20 • **Value: $27**

①

Aubergine
7.5" • #9107 • TJ
Issued: 1995 • Retired: 1998
Orig. Price: $12 • **Value: $20**

②

Auntie Adina (LE-500)
14" • N/A • N/A
Issued: N/A • Retired: N/A
Orig. Price: N/A • **Value: $230**

③

Auntie Babbit
12" • #91660 • JB
Issued: 1996 • Retired: 1998
Orig. Price: $30 • **Value: $40**

④

Auntie Harestein
14" • N/A • N/A
Issued: 1993 • Retired: 1993
Orig. Price: N/A • **Value: N/E**

⑤

Babs
12" • #5650-09 • BA
Issued: 1994 • Retired: 1998
Orig. Price: $16 • **Value: $30**

⑥

Baby
14" • #6105H • TJ
Issued: 1990 • Retired: 1991
Orig. Price: N/A • **Value: $265**

⑦
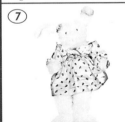
Beatrice
14" • #6168H • TJ
Issued: 1991 • Retired: 1991
Orig. Price: $63 • **Value: N/E**

⑧

Bedford Boneah
17" • #58291-05 • CH
Issued: 1998 • Current
Orig. Price: $23 • **Value: $23**

⑨

Beecher B. Bunny
10" • #5250-10 • JB
Issued: 1996 • Retired: 1998
Orig. Price: $16 • **Value: $30**

⑩

Bixie
12" • #56501-10 • BA
Issued: 1998 • Current
Orig. Price: $16 • **Value: $16**

HARES

	Price Paid	Value Of My Collection
1.		
2.		
3.		
4.		
5.		
6.		
7.		
8.		
9.		
10.		

PENCIL TOTALS

HARES

(1)

Bopper
14" • #5748 • HD
Issued: 1991 • Retired: 1992
Orig. Price: $27 • **Value: $145**

(2)

Brigette Delapain
10" • #91691 • TJ
Issued: 1996 • Retired: 1998
Orig. Price: $21 • **Value: $43**

(3)

Brigham Boneah
15" • #58291 • CH
Issued: 1997 • Current
Orig. Price: $23 • **Value: $23**

(4)

Briton R. Hare
15" • #5204 • JB
Issued: pre-1990 • Retired: 1991
Orig. Price: $20 • **Value: $100**

(5)

Bumpus
9" • #5746 • HD
Issued: 1991 • Retired: 1992
Orig. Price: $14 • **Value: $100**

(6)

Bunnylove Rarebit
9" • #91314 • TJ
Issued: 1996 • Retired: 1998
Orig. Price: $20 • **Value: $39**

HARES

	Price Paid	Value Of My Collection
1.		
2.		
3.		
4.		
5.		
6.		
7.		
8.		
9.		
10.		

✏ **PENCIL TOTALS**

(7)

Camilla
7.5" • #5732 • AS
Issued: 1993 • Retired: 1998
Orig. Price: $7 • **Value: $17**

(8)

Carlin Wabbit
8" • #9115 • TJ
Issued: 1995 • Retired: 1998
Orig. Price: $13 • **Value: $24**

(9)

Cecilia
8" • #5648-01 • BA
Issued: 1993 • Retired: 1998
Orig. Price: $11 • **Value: $19**

(10)

Chardonnay
7.5" • #9106 • TJ
Issued: 1995 • Retired: 1998
Orig. Price: $12 • **Value: $25**

①

Charlotte R. Hare
14" • #5224 • JB
Issued: 1992 • Retired: 1998
Orig. Price: $20 • **Value: $30**

②

Chelsea R. Hare
14" • #5217-01 • JB
Issued: 1993 • Retired: 1998
Orig. Price: $20 • **Value: $26**

③

Chesterfield Q. Burpee
8" • #91546 • TJ
Issued: 1996 • Retired: 1998
Orig. Price: $21 • **Value: $33**

④

Chloe Fitzhare
17" • #5240-03 • JB
Issued: 1996 • Retired: 1998
Orig. Price: $29 • **Value: $34**

⑤

Clara R. Hare
8" • #5227-08 • JB
Issued: 1994 • Retired: 1998
Orig. Price: $10 • **Value: $20**

⑥

Clarisse
16" • #91208 • TJ
Issued: 1997 • Retired: 1998
Orig. Price: $40 • **Value: $54**

⑦

Columbine Dubois
6" • #91402 • TJ
Issued: 1996 • Retired: 1998
Orig. Price: $12 • **Value: $22**

⑧

Cora B. Bunny
20" • #5212 • JB
Issued: pre-1990 • Retired: 1994
Orig. Price: $29 • **Value: $112**

⑨

Cordillia R. Hare
15" • #5205 • JB
Issued: pre-1990 • Retired: 1992
Orig. Price: $20 • **Value: $118**

⑩

Cosette D. Lapine
10" • #916601 • TJ
Issued: 1997 • Current
Orig. Price: $27 • **Value: $27**

HARES

	Price Paid	Value Of My Collection
1.		
2.		
3.		
4.		
5.		
6.		
7.		
8.		
9.		
10.		

PENCIL TOTALS

HARES

①

Cousin Rose Anjanette
7.5" • #91112-01 • TJ
Issued: 1998 • Current
Orig. Price: $12 • **Value: $12**

②

Curly Lapin
14" • #5207 • JB
Issued: pre-1990 • Retired: 1995
Orig. Price: $14 • **Value: $56**

③

Daffodil de la Hoppsack
8" • #91404 • TJ
Issued: 1998 • To Be Retired: 1999
Orig. Price: $13 • **Value: $13**

④

Daisey
12" • #9109 • TJ
Issued: 1995 • Retired: 1998
Orig. Price: $12 • **Value: $20**

⑤

Daphne R. Hare
14" • #5225 • JB
Issued: 1992 • Retired: 1998
Orig. Price: $20 • **Value: $35**

⑥

Darcy Babbit
14" • #9178 • TJ
Issued: 1993 • Retired: 1995
Orig. Price: $18 • **Value: $120**

Hares

	Price Paid	Value Of My Collection
1.		
2.		
3.		
4.		
5.		
6.		
7.		
8.		
9.		

⑦

PHOTO
UNAVAILABLE

Darcy Babbit II
info unavailable
Orig. Price: N/A • **Value: $135**

⑧

Delia R. Hare
12" • #5202 • JB
Issued: 1992 • Retired: 1992
Orig. Price: $14 • **Value: $125**

⑨

Demi
10.5" • #9112 • TJ
Issued: 1995 • Retired: 1998
Orig. Price: $20 • **Value: $35**

✏ PENCIL TOTALS

①

Demi II
12" • #9112-00 • TJ
Issued: 1995 • Retired: 1995
Orig. Price: $21 • **Value: $35**

②

Diana
10.5" • #5738 • AS
Issued: 1991 • Retired: 1997
Orig. Price: $14 • **Value: $38**

③

Diana
8" • #9181-01 • TJ
Issued: 1996 • Retired: 1997
Orig. Price: $21 • **Value: $29**

④

Diana
(also known as "Elizabeth")
7.5" • #98041 • TJ
Issued: 1996 • Retired: 1996
Orig. Price: $12 • **Value: $27**

⑤

Dixie
16" • #56541-08 • BA
Issued: 1996 • Retired: 1998
Orig. Price: $24 • **Value: $30**

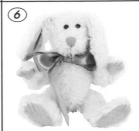

⑥

Dolly Q. Bunnycombe
10" • #590150-01 • MB
Issued: 1998 • Retired: 1998
Orig. Price: $24 • **Value: $40**

HARES

⑦

Donna
8" • #1200-01 • CC
Issued: 1994 • Retired: 1998
Orig. Price: $7 • **Value: $19**

⑧

Dora B. Bunny
20" • #5211 • JB
Issued: pre-1990 • Retired: 1994
Orig. Price: $29 • **Value: $160**

⑨ New!

Dudley Hopson
8" • #91663 • TJ
Issued: 1999 • Current
Orig. Price: $12 • **Value: $12**

⑩ New!

Earhart Harington
4.5" • #590086-01 • MB
Issued: 1999 • Current
Orig. Price: $10 • **Value: $10**

HARES

	Price Paid	Value Of My Collection
1.		
2.		
3.		
4.		
5.		
6.		
7.		
8.		
9.		
10.		
		PENCIL TOTALS

HARES

①

Edina Flatstein
8" • #5685-05 • FL
Issued: 1996 • Current
Orig. Price: $13 • **Value: $13**

②

New!

Edith Q. Harington
9" • #590160-03 • MB
Issued: 1999 • To Be Retired: 1999
Orig. Price: $26 • **Value: $26**

③

Eleanor
10.5" • #5737-01 • AS
Issued: 1995 • Retired: 1997
Orig. Price: $14 • **Value: $33**

④

Elizabeth
7.5" • #5733 • AS
Issued: 1991 • Current
Orig. Price: $7 • **Value: $7**

⑤

Eloise R. Hare
8.5" • #5230-10 • JB
Issued: 1994 • Current
Orig. Price: $12 • **Value: $12**

⑥

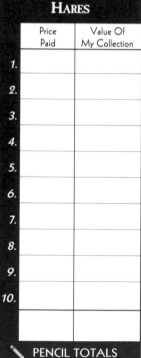

Elsinore
7.5" • #5732-05 • AS
Issued: 1996 • Current
Orig. Price: $7 • **Value: $7**

HARES

	Price Paid	Value Of My Collection
1.		
2.		
3.		
4.		
5.		
6.		
7.		
8.		
9.		
10.		

✏ PENCIL TOTALS

⑦

PHOTO UNAVAILABLE

Emily Babbit *(Spring 1993)*
8" • #9150 • TJ
Issued: 1993 • Retired: 1994
Orig. Price: $20 • **Value: $165**

⑧

Emily Babbit *(Fall 1993)*
8" • #9158 • TJ
Issued: 1993 • Retired: 1994
Orig. Price: $24 • **Value: $145**

⑨

Emily Babbit *(Spring 1994)*
10.5" • #9150 • TJ
Issued: 1994 • Retired: 1995
Orig. Price: $27 • **Value: $60**

⑩

Emily Babbit *(Spring 1995)*
10.5" • #9150-01 • TJ
Issued: 1995 • Retired: 1996
Orig. Price: $20 • **Value: $52**

①

Emily Babbit *(Fall 1995)*
10.5" • #9150-04 • TJ
Issued: 1995 • Retired: 1996
Orig. Price: $20 • **Value: $45**

②

Emily Babbit *(Spring 1996)*
10.5" • #9150-05 • TJ
Issued: 1996 • Retired: 1997
Orig. Price: $24 • **Value: $39**

③

Emily Babbit *(Fall 1996)*
8" • #9150-06 • TJ
Issued: 1996 • Retired: 1997
Orig. Price: $24 • **Value: $35**

④

Emily Babbit *(Spring 1997)*
10.5" • #9150-07 • TJ
Issued: 1997 • Retired: 1998
Orig. Price: $24 • **Value: $34**

⑤

Emily Babbit *(Fall 1997)*
10.5" • #9150-08 • TJ
Issued: 1997 • Retired: 1998
Orig. Price: $25 • **Value: $30**

⑥
Emily Babbit *(Spring 1998)*
8" • #9150-09 • TJ
Issued: 1998 • To Be Retired: 1999
Orig. Price: $27 • **Value: $27**

⑦

Emily Babbit *(Fall 1998)*
10" • #9150-10 • TJ
Issued: 1998 • To Be Retired: 1999
Orig. Price: $27 • **Value: $27**

⑧
New!

Emily Babbit *(Spring 1999)*
8" • #9150-11 • TJ
Issued: 1999 • Current
Orig. Price: $27 • **Value: $27**

⑨

Emily R. Hare
14" • #5226 • JB
Issued: 1992 • Retired: 1993
Orig. Price: $20 • **Value: $100**

⑩

Emma R. Hare
14" • #5225-08 • JB
Issued: 1994 • Retired: 1996
Orig. Price: $20 • **Value: $52**

HARES

HARES

	Price Paid	Value Of My Collection
1.		
2.		
3.		
4.		
5.		
6.		
7.		
8.		
9.		
10.		
PENCIL TOTALS		

①

Farnsworth Jr.
9.5" • #5870-08 • AR
Issued: 1995 • Retired: 1998
Orig. Price: $12 • **Value: $25**

②

Farnsworth Sr.
15" • #5875-08 • AR
Issued: 1995 • Retired: 1998
Orig. Price: $20 • **Value: $34**

③

Fergie
7.5" • #5735 • AS
Issued: 1991 • Retired: 1992
Orig. Price: $7 • **Value: $70**

④ **New!**

Fern Blumenshine
6" • #91692 • TJ
Issued: 1999 • Current
Orig. Price: $12 • **Value: $12**

⑤

Fleurette Hare
info unavailable
Orig. Price: N/A • **Value: N/E**

⑥

Flora B. Bunny
20" • #5210 • JB
Issued: 1990 • Retired: 1994
Orig. Price: $29 • **Value: $104**

HARES

	Price Paid	Value Of My Collection
1.		
2.		
3.		
4.		
5.		
6.		
7.		
8.		
9.		
10.		

 PENCIL TOTALS

⑦ **New!**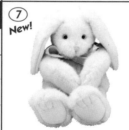

Flossie B. Hopplebuns
8" • #56481-10 • BA
Issued: 1999 • Current
Orig. Price: $11 • **Value: $11**

⑧

Frangelica
12" • #9109-10 • TJ
Issued: 1996 • Retired: 1998
Orig. Price: $12 • **Value: $27**

⑨

G.G. Willikers
8" • #91162 • TJ
Issued: 1996 • Retired: 1998
Orig. Price: $20 • **Value: $37**

⑩

Gardner
N/A • #6162H • TJ
Issued: 1991 • Retired: 1991
Orig. Price: $63 • **Value: N/E**

1

Giselle de la Fleur
6" • #91703 • TJ
Issued: 1998 • Current
Orig. Price: $10 • **Value: $10**

2

Golda
10.5" • #9146 • TJ
Issued: 1994 • Retired: 1995
Orig. Price: $20 • **Value: $42**

3

PHOTO
UNAVAILABLE

Grace
N/A • #6163H • TJ
Issued: 1991 • Retired: 1991
Orig. Price: $63 • **Value: N/E**

4

Grace Agnes
11" • #5830-01 • CB
Issued: 1994 • Retired: 1995
Orig. Price: $21 • **Value: $72**

5

Grayson R. Hare
9" • #5230-06 • JB
Issued: 1997 • Current
Orig. Price: $12 • **Value: $12**

6

New!

Greta de la Fleur
6" • #91704 • TJ
Issued: 1999 • Current
Orig. Price: $9 • **Value: $9**

7

Gretchen
10" • #911210 • TJ
Issued: 1998 • To Be Retired: 1999
Orig. Price: $17 • **Value: $17**

8

Hailey
8" • #9168 • TJ
Issued: 1995 • Retired: 1998
Orig. Price: $11 • **Value: $20**

9

Hannah
7.5" • #91111 • TJ
Issued: 1997 • To Be Retired: 1999
Orig. Price: $12 • **Value: $12**

10

Harriett R. Hare
12" • #5200-08 • JB
Issued: 1994 • Retired: 1996
Orig. Price: $14 • **Value: $43**

HARES

	Price Paid	Value Of My Collection
1.		
2.		
3.		
4.		
5.		
6.		
7.		
8.		
9.		
10.		
PENCIL TOTALS		

HARES

(1)

Harry Lapin II
14" • #5217 • JB
Issued: 1992 • Retired: 1993
Orig. Price: N/A • **Value: $190**

(2)

Harry R. Hare
17" • #5217-03 • JB
Issued: 1993 • Retired: 1994
Orig. Price: $20 • **Value: $115**

(3) New!

Harvey P. Hoppleby
9" • #51740 • BY
Issued: 1999 • Current
Orig. Price: $8 • **Value: $8**

(4)

Hedy
10.5" • #9186-01 • TJ
Issued: 1994 • Retired: 1998
Orig. Price: $20 • **Value: $38**

(5)

Higgins
10" • #5877-06 • AR
Issued: 1995 • Retired: 1997
Orig. Price: $21 • **Value: $45**

(6)

Higgy
7" • #5876-03 • AR
Issued: 1996 • Retired: 1997
Orig. Price: $20 • **Value: $32**

HARES

	Price Paid	Value Of My Collection
1.		
2.		
3.		
4.		
5.		
6.		
7.		
8.		
9.		
10.		
PENCIL TOTALS		

(7)

PHOTO UNAVAILABLE

Homer
N/A • #6166H • TJ
Issued: 1991 • Retired: 1991
Orig. Price: $63 • **Value: N/E**

(8)

Hopkins
10.5" • #91121 • TJ
Issued: 1998 • To Be Retired: 1999
Orig. Price: $18 • **Value: $18**

(9) New!

Iris Rosenbunny
10" • #91651 • TJ
Issued: 1999 • Current
Orig. Price: $20 • **Value: $20**

(10)

Jack
20" • #5215 • JB
Issued: 1991 • Retired: 1992
Orig. Price: $29 • **Value: $185**

(1)

Jane
14" • #5732 • AS
Issued: 1992 • Retired: 1992
Orig. Price: $20 • **Value: $205**

(2)

Jane
10.5" • #5737-05 • AS
Issued: 1994 • Retired: 1998
Orig. Price: $14 • **Value: $22**

(3)

Janet
8" • #1200-03 • CC
Issued: 1994 • Retired: 1997
Orig. Price: $7 • **Value: $30**

(4)

Jessica
8" • #9168-02 • TJ
Issued: 1997 • Current
Orig. Price: $12 • **Value: $12**

(5)

PHOTO
UNAVAILABLE

Jill
20" • #5216 • JB
Issued: 1991 • Retired: 1992
Orig. Price: $29 • **Value: $170**

(6)

Josephine
6" • #91701 • TJ
Issued: 1996 • Retired: 1998
Orig. Price: $9 • **Value: $15**

(7)

New!

Juliana Hopkins
8" • #91122 • TJ
Issued: 1999 • Current
Orig. Price: $17 • **Value: $17**

(8)

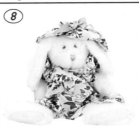

Julip O'Harea
12" • #91664 • TJ
Issued: 1996 • Retired: 1998
Orig. Price: $23 • **Value: $28**

(9)

Katerina
10" • #5874 • HT
Issued: 1992 • Retired: 1993
Orig. Price: $20 • **Value: $90**

(10)

Kathryn
7.5" • #5732-01 • AS
Issued: 1994 • Retired: 1998
Orig. Price: $7 • **Value: $17**

HARES

HARES

	Price Paid	Value Of My Collection
1.		
2.		
3.		
4.		
5.		
6.		
7.		
8.		
9.		
10.		

PENCIL TOTALS

① New!

Kerry Q. Hopgood
17" • #52401-03 • JB
Issued: 1999 • Current
Orig. Price: $29 • **Value: $29**

②

Lacy
14" • #6100H • TJ
Issued: 1990 • Retired: 1994
Orig. Price: $16 • **Value: $100**

③

Lacy
17" • #6101H • TJ
Issued: 1990 • Retired: 1992
Orig. Price: $21 • **Value: $105**

④ New!

Lady Harriwell
11" • #91892-14 • TJ
Issued: 1999 • Current
Orig. Price: $21 • **Value: $21**

⑤

Lady Payton
10.5" • #918921-09 • TJ
Issued: 1998 • Current
Orig. Price: $17 • **Value: $17**

⑥

Lady Pembrooke
15" • #91892-09 • TJ
Issued: 1997 • To Be Retired: 1999
Orig. Price: $21 • **Value: $21**

HARES

	Price Paid	Value Of My Collection
1.		
2.		
3.		
4.		
5.		
6.		
7.		
8.		
9.		
10.		
PENCIL TOTALS		

⑦

Lana
10.5" • #9186 • TJ
Issued: 1993 • Retired: 1994
Orig. Price: $20 • **Value: $50**

⑧

Larry Lapin
17" • #5209 • JB
Issued: pre-1990 • Retired: 1991
Orig. Price: $20 • **Value: $160**

⑨

PHOTO UNAVAILABLE

Larry Too
17" • #5217 • JB
Issued: 1992 • Retired: 1992
Orig. Price: $20 • **Value: N/E**

⑩

Lauren
8" • #9168-01 • TJ
Issued: 1996 • Retired: 1998
Orig. Price: $11 • **Value: $22**

①

Lavinia V. Hariweather
10" • #91661 • TJ
Issued: 1997 • Current
Orig. Price: $20 • **Value: $20**

②

Lenora Flatstein
8" • #5685-08 • FL
Issued: 1994 • Retired: 1998
Orig. Price: $12 • **Value: $25**

③

Leona B. Bunny
20" • #5214 • JB
Issued: pre-1990 • Retired: 1992
Orig. Price: $29 • **Value: N/E**

④ New!

Libby Lapinette
6" • #91681 • TJ
Issued: 1999 • Current
Orig. Price: $11 • **Value: $11**

⑤

Lily R. Hare
8" • #5227-01 • JB
Issued: 1994 • Current
Orig. Price: $10 • **Value: $10**

⑥

Livingston R. Hare
12" • #5200 • JB
Issued: pre-1990 • Retired: 1998
Orig. Price: $14 • **Value: $25**

⑦

Lucille
13.5" • #91141 • TJ
Issued: 1997 • Retired: 1998
Orig. Price: $24 • **Value: $40**

⑧ New!

Lucinda de la Fleur
6" • #91705 • TJ
Issued: 1999 • Current
Orig. Price: $9 • **Value: $9**

⑨

Lucy P. Blumenshine
6" • #91702 • TJ
Issued: 1997 • Retired: 1998
Orig. Price: $10 • **Value: $20**

⑩

Magnolia O'Harea
17" • #91667 • TJ
Issued: 1996 • Retired: 1998
Orig. Price: $31 • **Value: $38**

HARES

HARES

	Price Paid	Value Of My Collection
1.		
2.		
3.		
4.		
5.		
6.		
7.		
8.		
9.		
10.		
PENCIL TOTALS		

①

Mallory
info unavailable
Orig. Price: N/A • **Value: $35**

②

Margaret Mary
11" • #5830 • CB
Issued: 1992 • Retired: 1995
Orig. Price: $21 • **Value: $82**

③ New!

Marigold McHare
8" • #52270-08 • JB
Issued: 1999 • Current
Orig. Price: $10 • **Value: $10**

④

Marlena
10.5" • #9154 • TJ
Issued: 1994 • Retired: 1997
Orig. Price: $20 • **Value: $37**

⑤

Marta M. Hare
12" • #5206 • JB
Issued: pre-1990 • Retired: 1992
Orig. Price: $14 • **Value: $130**

⑥

Martha T. Bunnycombe
15.5" • #590140-03 • MB
Issued: 1998 • Retired: 1998
Orig. Price: $51 • **Value: $66**

HARES

	Price Paid	Value Of My Collection
1.		
2.		
3.		
4.		
5.		
6.		
7.		
8.		
9.		
10.		

✎ **PENCIL TOTALS**

⑦

Mary
10.5" • #5737 • AS
Issued: 1991 • Retired: 1997
Orig. Price: $14 • **Value: $28**

⑧

Mary Catherine
9" • #5829 • CB
Issued: 1992 • Retired: 1995
Orig. Price: $16 • **Value: $65**

⑨

Mary Regina
9" • #5829-01 • CB
Issued: 1994 • Retired: 1995
Orig. Price: $16 • **Value: $65**

⑩ PHOTO UNAVAILABLE

Matilda
N/A • #6161H • TJ
Issued: 1991 • Retired: 1991
Orig. Price: $63 • **Value: N/E**

(1)

PHOTO
UNAVAILABLE

Merlin
N/A • #6167H • TJ
Issued: 1991 • Retired: 1991
Orig. Price: $63 • **Value: N/E**

(2)

Michelline
7.5" • #91815 • TJ
Issued: 1996 • Retired: 1997
Orig. Price: $13 • **Value: $25**

(3)

Mickey
8" • #1200-08 • CC
Issued: 1994 • Retired: 1995
Orig. Price: $7 • **Value: $50**

(4)

Mickie
16" • #5654 • BA
Issued: 1992 • Retired: 1998
Orig. Price: $21 • **Value: N/E**

(5) New!

Millie Hopkins
8" • #91123 • TJ
Issued: 1999 • Current
Orig. Price: $18 • **Value: $18**

(6)

Mimi Delapain
8" • #9169 • JB
Issued: 1995 • Retired: 1998
Orig. Price: $9 • **Value: $19**

(7)

Mimosa
17" • #9110-10 • TJ
Issued: 1996 • Retired: 1998
Orig. Price: $19 • **Value: $28**

(8) New!

Miranda Blumenshine
10" • #91142 • TJ
Issued: 1999 • Current
Orig. Price: $23 • **Value: $23**

(9)

Moe Lapin
14" • #5208 • JB
Issued: 1990 • Retired: 1995
Orig. Price: $14 • **Value: $52**

(10)

Molly
14" • N/A • N/A
Issued: 1993 • Retired: 1993
Orig. Price: N/A • **Value: N/E**

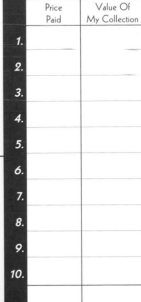

HARES

	Price Paid	Value Of My Collection
1.		
2.		
3.		
4.		
5.		
6.		
7.		
8.		
9.		
10.		

PENCIL TOTALS

HARES

① Momma O'Harea & Bonnie Blue

12" & 6" • #91008 • TJ
Issued: 1998 • Retired: 1998
Orig. Price: $29 • **Value: $34**

② Montgomery Flatstein

8" • #5685-10 • FL
Issued: 1994 • Current
Orig. Price: $12 • **Value: $13**

③ Mrs. Harelwig

PHOTO UNAVAILABLE
info unavailable
Orig. Price: N/A • **Value: N/E**

④ Mrs. Harestein

PHOTO UNAVAILABLE
info unavailable
Orig. Price: N/A • **Value: N/E**

⑤ Nanny II

PHOTO UNAVAILABLE
info unavailable
Orig. Price: N/A • **Value: N/E**

⑥ Natasha

10" • #5873 • HT
Issued: 1992 • Retired: 1994
Orig. Price: $20 • **Value: $80**

HARES

✎ PENCIL TOTALS

⑦ Nickie

PHOTO UNAVAILABLE
16" • #5653 • BA
Issued: 1992 • Retired: 1993
Orig. Price: $21 • **Value: $46**

⑧ Olga

6" • #5871 • HT
Issued: 1992 • Retired: 1992
Orig. Price: $9 • **Value: $90**

⑨ Oliver

6" • #91110 • TJ
Issued: 1998 • Current
Orig. Price: $12 • **Value: $12**

⑩ Orchid de la Hoppsack

8" • #91405 • TJ
Issued: 1998 • To Be Retired: 1999
Orig. Price: $13 • **Value: $13**

① New!

Pansy Rosenbunny
10" • #91652 • TJ
Issued: 1999 • Current
Orig. Price: $20 • **Value: $20**

②

Peapod
6" • #91071 • TJ
Issued: 1996 • Retired: 1997
Orig. Price: $12 • **Value: $35**

③

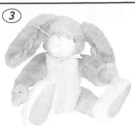

Penelope
14" • #5729 • AS
Issued: 1992 • Retired: 1995
Orig. Price: $20 • **Value: $65**

④

Peter
6" • #9111 • TJ
Issued: 1995 • Retired: 1997
Orig. Price: $11 • **Value: $28**

⑤

Pixie
12" • #5651 • BA
Issued: 1992 • Retired: 1993
Orig. Price: $16 • **Value: $52**

⑥

Pixie
12" • #56510-05 • BA
Issued: 1998 • Current
Orig. Price: $16 • **Value: $16**

⑦

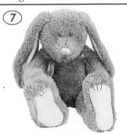

Priscilla R. Hare
14" • #5217-08 • JB
Issued: 1995 • Retired: 1997
Orig. Price: $16 • **Value: $30**

⑧

Priscilla R. Hare
17" • #5217-12 • JB
Issued: 1993 • Retired: 1994
Orig. Price: $20 • **Value: N/E**

⑨

Regina
14" • #5731 • AS
Issued: 1991 • Retired: 1993
Orig. Price: $20 • **Value: $135**

⑩

Regina
10.5" • #5737-08 • AS
Issued: 1998 • Current
Orig. Price: $14 • **Value: $14**

HARES

	Price Paid	Value Of My Collection
1.		
2.		
3.		
4.		
5.		
6.		
7.		
8.		
9.		
10.		

PENCIL TOTALS

HARES

① 	② New! 	③ New! 
Rita	**Rosalynn P. Harington**	**Roscoe P. Bumpercrop**
11" • #1201-08 • CC	12" • #590140-01 • MB	17" • #912079 • TJ
Issued: 1994 • Retired: 1995	Issued: 1999 • To Be Retired: 1999	Issued: 1999 • Current
Orig. Price: $10 • **Value: $57**	Orig. Price: $51 • **Value: $51**	Orig. Price: $40 • **Value: $40**
④ 	⑤ 	⑥ PHOTO UNAVAILABLE
Rose	**Roxbunny R. Hare**	**Royce**
7.5" • #91112 • TJ	14" • #5878-06 • AR	N/A • #6107H • TJ
Issued: 1997 • Retired: 1998	Issued: 1997 • Retired: 1998	Issued: 1990 • Retired: 1992
Orig. Price: $12 • **Value: $19**	Orig. Price: $14 • **Value: $28**	Orig. Price: $32 • **Value: $300**

HARES

	Price Paid	Value Of My Collection
1.		
2.		
3.		
4.		
5.		
6.		
7.		
8.		
9.		
10.		

✏ **PENCIL TOTALS**

⑦

Rumpus
9" • #5745 • HD
Issued: 1991 • Retired: 1992
Orig. Price: $14 • **Value: $130**

⑧

Ruth
11" • #1201-01 • CC
Issued: 1994 • Retired: 1995
Orig. Price: $10 • **Value: $55**

⑨

Sangria
17" • #9110-05 • TJ
Issued: 1998 • Current
Orig. Price: $20 • **Value: $20**

⑩

Sara
7.5" • #9140 • TJ
Issued: 1994 • Retired: 1996
Orig. Price: $13 • **Value: $50**

(1)

Sara II
6" • #91401 • TJ
Issued: 1996 • Retired: 1998
Orig. Price: $13 • **Value: $18**

(2)

Sarah
10.5" • #5739 • AS
Issued: 1991 • Retired: 1993
Orig. Price: $14 • **Value: $67**

(3)

Sharona
10.5" • #5737-10 • AS
Issued: 1998 • Current
Orig. Price: $14 • **Value: $14**

(4)

Sophie
12" • #9114 • TJ
Issued: 1995 • Retired: 1998
Orig. Price: $20 • **Value: $32**

(5)

Sophie B. Bunny
20" • #5215 • JB
Issued: 1993 • Retired: 1994
Orig. Price: $29 • **Value: $210**

(6)

Squeeky
8" • #5620 • SQ
Issued: 1991 • Retired: 1992
Orig. Price: $10 • **Value: $85**

(7)

Squeeky
8" • #5621 • SQ
Issued: 1992 • Retired: 1992
Orig. Price: $10 • **Value: $92**

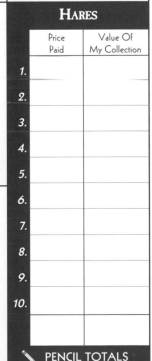

(8)

Stanley R. Hare
12" • #5201 • JB
Issued: 1991 • Retired: 1998
Orig. Price: $14 • **Value: $23**

(9)

Stewart Rarebit
8" • #9116 • TJ
Issued: 1995 • Retired: 1998
Orig. Price: $13 • **Value: $20**

(10) New!

Taffy C. Hopplebuns
8" • #56481-03 • BA
Issued: 1999 • Current
Orig. Price: $11 • **Value: $11**

HARES

	Price Paid	Value Of My Collection
1.		
2.		
3.		
4.		
5.		
6.		
7.		
8.		
9.		
10.		

✏ **PENCIL TOTALS**

HARES

New!

Tami F. Wuzzie
3" • #596100 • TF
Issued: 1999 • Current
Orig. Price: $8 • **Value: $8**

Tanner F. Wuzzie
4" • #595300-08 • TF
Issued: 1998 • Current
Orig. Price: $7 • **Value: $7**

New!

Tapper F. Wuzzie
3" • #595300-06 • TF
Issued: 1999 • Current
Orig. Price: $7 • **Value: $7**

Tarragon
17" • #9110-07 • TJ
Issued: 1996 • Retired: 1997
Orig. Price: $19 • **Value: $45**

Tatiana
14" • #5877 • HT
Issued: 1992 • Retired: 1992
Orig. Price: $32 • **Value: $140**

Teddy Hare
info unavailable
Orig. Price: $13 • **Value: N/E**

HARES

	Price Paid	Value Of My Collection
1.		
2.		
3.		
4.		
5.		
6.		
7.		
8.		
9.		

Teddy Hare
info unavailable
Orig. Price: N/A • **Value: N/E**

Teddy Hare
info unavailable
Orig. Price: N/A • **Value: N/E**

Teddy Hare
info unavailable
Orig. Price: N/A • **Value: N/E**

① Thump

14" • #5747 • HD
Issued: 1991 • Retired: 1992
Orig. Price: $27 • **Value: $170**

② Tipper

8" • #5648-08 • BA
Issued: 1993 • Retired: 1997
Orig. Price: $11 • **Value: $35**

③ Tippy F. Wuzzie

4" • #595300-01 • TF
Issued: 1998 • Current
Orig. Price: $7 • **Value: $7**

④ Trixie

16" • #5654-08 • BA
Issued: 1993 • Retired: 1996
Orig. Price: $24 • **Value: $82**

⑤ Tutu
New!

PHOTO UNAVAILABLE
N/A • #6169H • TJ
Issued: 1991 • Retired: 1991
Orig. Price: $63 • **Value: N/E**

⑥ Vanessa D. LaPinne

10" • #91662 • TJ
Issued: 1999 • Current
Orig. Price: $27 • **Value: $27**

⑦ Veronica

10.5" • #9181 • TJ
Issued: 1994 • Retired: 1997
Orig. Price: $20 • **Value: $44**

⑧ Victoria

7.5" • #5736 • AS
Issued: 1991 • Current
Orig. Price: $7 • **Value: $7**

⑨ Violet Dubois

6" • #91403 • TJ
Issued: 1996 • Retired: 1998
Orig. Price: $12 • **Value: $20**

⑩ Wedgewood J. Hopgood
New!

17" • #52401-10 • JB
Issued: 1999 • Current
Orig. Price: $29 • **Value: $29**

HARES

	Price Paid	Value Of My Collection
1.		
2.		
3.		
4.		
5.		
6.		
7.		
8.		
9.		
10.		

PENCIL TOTALS

HARES

①

Whitney
12" • #9130 • TJ
Issued: 1995 • Retired: 1998
Orig. Price: $20 • **Value: $26**

②

Wilhelm Von Bruin
6" • #5015 • WB
Issued: 1992 • Retired: 1995
Orig. Price: $9 • **Value: $42**

③

Wixie
12" • #5650 • BA
Issued: 1992 • Retired: 1998
Orig. Price: $16 • **Value: $23**

④

Zelda Fitzhare
17" • #5240-10 • JB
Issued: 1995 • Retired: 1998
Orig. Price: $29 • **Value: $32**

LAMBS

With names such as the distinctive "Tallulah Baahead" and the gruff "Dick Butkus," this branch of the family tree came into the collection like a lion. However, they left like a lamb as all but two have slipped quietly into retirement.

HARES

	Price Paid	Value Of My Collection
1.		
2.		
3.		
4.		

LAMBS

5.		
6.		
7.		
8.		

✏ PENCIL TOTALS

⑤

Abbey Ewe
14" • #91311-01 • TJ
Issued: 1996 • Retired: 1998
Orig. Price: $29 • **Value: $37**

⑥

Daisy Ewe
10" • #5500 • AM
Issued: pre-1990 • Retired: 1994
Orig. Price: $14 • **Value: $50**

⑦

Dick Butkus
10" • #9155 • TJ
Issued: 1994 • Retired: 1994
Orig. Price: $20 • **Value: $118**

⑧

Elspethe Ewe
8" • #91312 • TJ
Issued: 1997 • Retired: 1998
Orig. Price: $11 • **Value: $21**

(1)

Madabout Ewe
6" • #91312-01 • TJ
Issued: 1998 • Current
Orig. Price: $11 • **Value: $11**

(2)

Maisey Ewe
10" • #5501 • AM
Issued: pre-1990 • Retired: 1994
Orig. Price: $14 • **Value: $78**

(3)

Maude Ewe
7" • #5510-07 • AM
Issued: 1994 • Retired: 1996
Orig. Price: $7 • **Value: $45**

(4)

McNeil Mutton
14" • #91311-07 • TJ
Issued: 1996 • Retired: 1998
Orig. Price: $29 • **Value: $34**

(5)

Pansy
10" • #5501-01 • N/A
Issued: N/A • Retired: N/A
Orig. Price: N/A • **Value: $87**

(6)

Phoebe Ewe
7" • #5510-01 • AM
Issued: 1994 • Retired: 1996
Orig. Price: $7 • **Value: $43**

(7)

Rose Mutton
15" • #5520 • AM
Issued: pre-1990 • Retired: 1994
Orig. Price: $20 • **Value: $120**

(8)

Sadie Ewe
7" • #5510-03 • AM
Issued: 1994 • Retired: 1994
Orig. Price: $7 • **Value: $87**

(9)

Squeeky
8" • #5622 • SQ
Issued: 1992 • Retired: 1992
Orig. Price: $10 • **Value: $78**

(10)

Tallulah Baahead
14" • #5520-01 • AM
Issued: 1995 • Retired: 1998
Orig. Price: $20 • **Value: $30**

LAMBS (side tab)

LAMBS

	Price Paid	Value Of My Collection
1.		
2.		
3.		
4.		
5.		
6.		
7.		
8.		
9.		
10.		

✎ PENCIL TOTALS

①

PHOTO UNAVAILABLE

Tutu
N/A • #6169L • TJ
Issued: 1991 • Retired: 1991
Orig. Price: $63 • **Value: N/E**

②

Violet Ewe
10" • #5500-07 • AM
Issued: 1996 • Retired: 1998
Orig. Price: $14 • **Value: $28**

③

New!

Wannabee Ewe-Too
8" • #91312-02 • TJ
Issued: 1999 • Current
Orig. Price: $11 • **Value: $11**

LIONS

The Boyds lions' den consists of eight mighty warriors. However, the older, larger pieces (including "Elvis" who was once "king" of this jungle) have all been retired, leaving only "Dickie The Lionheart" and "Lance" to rule the forest.

④

Butch
8" • #5861 • BB
Issued: 1994 • Retired: 1994
Orig. Price: $14 • **Value: $100**

LAMBS

	Price Paid	Value Of My Collection
1.		
2.		
3.		

LIONS

4.		
5.		
6.		
7.		
8.		

✏ **PENCIL TOTALS**

⑤

Dickie The Lionheart
6" • #51700 • BY
Issued: 1997 • Current
Orig. Price: $5 • **Value: $5**

⑥

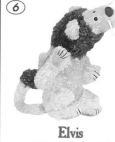

Elvis
12" • #5859 • AR
Issued: 1995 • Retired: 1996
Orig. Price: $20 • **Value: $40**

⑦

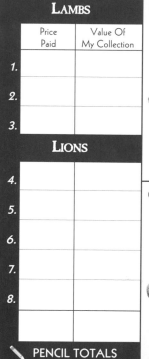

Lance
8" • #51900 • BY
Issued: 1997 • Current
Orig. Price: $8 • **Value: $8**

⑧

Leopold Q. Lion
10" • #5530 • AM
Issued: pre-1990 • Retired: 1993
Orig. Price: $14 • **Value: $145**

①

PHOTO
UNAVAILABLE

Merlin
info unavailable
Orig. Price: N/A • **Value: N/E**

②

Sampson T. Lion
14" • #5531 • AM
Issued: pre-1990 • Retired: 1992
Orig. Price: $29 • **Value: $250**

③

Spike T. Lion
14" • #5860 • BB
Issued: 1992 • Retired: 1994
Orig. Price: $20 • **Value: $100**

MICE

Since this category made its debut, 13 mice have joined the family. After a short break in 1996 and 1997, two mice were produced in 1998 and another two in 1999. With the exception of the festive Christmas mice, "Joy" and "Noel," the names of these critters are quite cheesy.

④

Bebe
6" • #9167 • TJ
Issued: 1994 • Retired: 1996
Orig. Price: $13 • **Value: $44**

⑤

Bebe
6" • #9167-01 • TJ
Issued: 1994 • Retired: 1995
Orig. Price: $13 • **Value: $44**

⑥

Brie
6" • #5756 • AS
Issued: 1993 • Current
Orig. Price: $8 • **Value: $8**

⑦

Chedda
6" • #5756-06 • AS
Issued: 1993 • Current
Orig. Price: $8 • **Value: $8**

⑧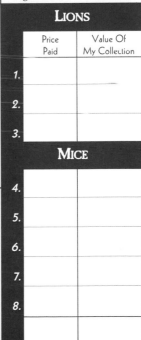

Colby S. Mouski
6" • #91672 • TJ
Issued: 1998 • Current
Orig. Price: $12 • **Value: $12**

LIONS

	Price Paid	Value Of My Collection
1.		
2.		
3.		

MICE

4.		
5.		
6.		
7.		
8.		

PENCIL TOTALS

LIONS/MICE

① New!

Cottage McNibble
6" • #91673 • TJ
Issued: 1999 • Current
Orig. Price: $12 • **Value: $12**

②

Feta
6" • #91075 • TJ
Issued: 1995 • Retired: 1996
Orig. Price: $12 • **Value: $47**

③

Gouda
6" • #91671 • TJ
Issued: 1998 • Current
Orig. Price: $12 • **Value: $12**

④

Joy
6" • #9165-06 • TJ
Issued: 1993 • Retired: 1996
Orig. Price: $12 • **Value: $32**

⑤

Noel
6" • #9165-01 • TJ
Issued: 1993 • Retired: 1996
Orig. Price: $12 • **Value: $32**

⑥

Roq
8" • #5757-01 • AS
Issued: 1994 • Retired: 1995
Orig. Price: $14 • **Value: $44**

MICE

	Price Paid	Value Of My Collection
1.		
2.		
3.		
4.		
5.		
6.		
7.		
8.		

✏ PENCIL TOTALS

⑦ New!

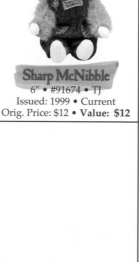

Sharp McNibble
6" • #91674 • TJ
Issued: 1999 • Current
Orig. Price: $12 • **Value: $12**

⑧

Stilton
8" • #5757 • AS
Issued: 1993 • Retired: 1995
Orig. Price: $14 • **Value: $47**

MONKEYS

The Simiansky family climbed into the Boyds family tree in 1993 and sought an early retirement before any more of their relatives could arrive. In 1997, however, the Tsuris brothers moved into the jungle and were joined the following year by the Monkbury clan.

Bertha S. Simiansky
10" • #5524-11 • AM
Issued: 1993 • Retired: 1996
Orig. Price: $14 • **Value: $35**

Dalton Monkbury
8" • #55242-08 • AM
Issued: 1998 • Current
Orig. Price: $12 • **Value: $12**

Darwin Monkbury
8" • #55242-05 • AM
Issued: 1998 • Current
Orig. Price: $12 • **Value: $12**

Finster R. Tsuris
10" • #55241-05 • AM
Issued: 1997 • Current
Orig. Price: $14 • **Value: $14**

Imogene R. Tsuris
10" • #55241-11 • AM
Issued: 1997 • Current
Orig. Price: $14 • **Value: $14**

Simon S. Simiansky
10" • #5524-10 • AM
Issued: 1993 • Retired: 1996
Orig. Price: $14 • **Value: $45**

MONKEYS

	Price Paid	Value Of My Collection
1.		
2.		
3.		
4.		
5.		
6.		

PENCIL TOTALS

MONKEYS

MOOSE

Over the years, this branch of the plush family has racked up 34 members, most of which have already retired. Here, collectors have the opportunity to meet the prestigious Von Hindenmoose family, as well as a variety of well-dressed characters with equally distinctive names.

Beatrice Von Hindenmoose
17" • #5542 • NL
Issued: 1991 • Retired: 1997
Orig. Price: $16 • **Value: $38**

Bismark Von Hindenmoose
20" • #5545-05 • NL
Issued: 1995 • Retired: 1996
Orig. Price: $29 • **Value: $62**

Edwina
14" • #9144 • TJ
Issued: 1994 • Retired: 1997
Orig. Price: $20 • **Value: $34**

Egon Von Hindenmoose
6" • #5546 • NL
Issued: 1993 • Retired: 1997
Orig. Price: $8 • **Value: $37**

MOOSE

	Price Paid	Value Of My Collection
1.		
2.		
3.		
4.		
5.		
6.		
7.		

✎ PENCIL TOTALS

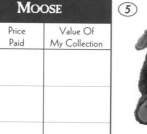

Euphoria
8" • #91446 • TJ
Issued: 1995 • Retired: 1998
Orig. Price: $14 • **Value: $25**

Father Krismoose
info unavailable
Orig. Price: N/A • **Value: N/E**

PHOTO UNAVAILABLE

Father Moose Moss
info unavailable
Orig. Price: N/A • **Value: N/E**

1

Father Moosemas
info unavailable
Orig. Price: N/A • **Value: N/E**

2

Festus
14" • #91444 • TJ
Issued: 1995 • Retired: 1996
Orig. Price: $21 • **Value: $50**

3

Gertrude
17" • #6108 • TJ
Issued: 1993 • Retired: 1993
Orig. Price: N/A • **Value: $240**

4

Helmut
14" • #9145 • TJ
Issued: 1994 • Retired: 1995
Orig. Price: $27 • **Value: $60**
Variation: green sweater
Value: $70

5

Justina
(formerly "Philomena")
14" • #91443 • TJ
Issued: 1995 • Retired: 1997
Orig. Price: $27 • **Value: $40**

6

Kris Moose
(formerly "Father Krismoose")
14" • #9192 • JB
Issued: 1992 • Retired: 1996
Orig. Price: $27 • **Value: $320**

7

PHOTO
UNAVAILABLE

Krismoose
info unavailable
Orig. Price: N/A • **Value: N/E**

8

Manheim Von Hindenmoose
20" • #5545 • NL
Issued: 1992 • Retired: 1996
Orig. Price: $29 • **Value: $63**

9

Martini
12" • #91109 • TJ
Issued: 1998 • Current
Orig. Price: $12 • **Value: $12**

MOOSE		
	Price Paid	Value Of My Collection
1.		
2.		
3.		
4.		
5.		
6.		
7.		
8.		
9.		
PENCIL TOTALS		

① Maurice Von Hindenmoose
14" • #5540-05 • NL
Issued: 1996 • Current
Orig. Price: $14 • **Value: $14**

② Maynard Von Hindenmoose
14" • #5541 • NL
Issued: 1992 • Retired: 1997
Orig. Price: $14 • **Value: $40**

③ Menachem
8.5" • #91212 • TJ
Issued: 1996 • Retired: 1998
Orig. Price: $20 • **Value: $28**

④ Mendel Von Hindenmoose
6" • #5547 • NL
Issued: 1996 • Current
Orig. Price: $8 • **Value: $8**

⑤ Miliken Von Hindenmoose
17" • #55421-05 • NL
Issued: 1997 • Current
Orig. Price: $20 • **Value: $20**

⑥ Millie LaMoose
9" • #51730 • BY
Issued: 1998 • Current
Orig. Price: $8 • **Value: $8**

MOOSE

	Price Paid	Value Of My Collection
1.		
2.		
3.		
4.		
5.		
6.		
7.		
8.		
9.		

✎ PENCIL TOTALS

⑦ Minney Moose
14" • #91108 • TJ
Issued: 1996 • Retired: 1998
Orig. Price: $20 • **Value: $29**

⑧ Montague
8" • #9121 • TJ
Issued: 1994 • Retired: 1996
Orig. Price: $20 • **Value: $39**

⑨ Monte Mooselton
12" • #917290 • TJ
Issued: 1998 • Current
Orig. Price: $21 • **Value: $21**

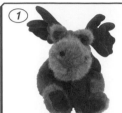

Mortimer Von Hindenmoose
14" • #55411-05 • NL
Issued: 1997 • Current
Orig. Price: $14 • **Value: $14**

Mother Moosemas
info unavailable
Orig. Price: N/A • **Value: N/E**

Murgatroyd Von Hindenmoose
14" • #5540 • NL
Issued: 1991 • Retired: 1994
Orig. Price: $14 • **Value: $38**

Murgatroyd Von Hindenmoose II
14" • #5540 • NL
Issued: 1993 • Retired: 1997
Orig. Price: $14 • **Value: $48**

Myron Von Hindenmoose
10" • #912121 • TJ
Issued: 1997 • Retired: 1998
Orig. Price: $21 • **Value: $30**

Nadia Von Hindenmoose
17" • #5542-01 • NL
Issued: 1994 • Retired: 1996
Orig. Price: $20 • **Value: $65**

Siegfried Von Hindenmoose
20" • #5544 • NL
Issued: 1991 • Retired: 1995
Orig. Price: $29 • **Value: $170**

Talbot F. Wuzzie
3.5" • #595440 • TF
Issued: 1998 • Current
Orig. Price: $7 • **Value: $7**

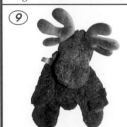

Windberg
8" • #5675-05 • FL
Issued: 1995 • Current
Orig. Price: $13 • **Value: $13**

MOOSE

	Price Paid	Value Of My Collection
1.		
2.		
3.		
4.		
5.		
6.		
7.		
8.		
9.		
✎ PENCIL TOTALS		

MOOSE

PIGS

While swine have been a part of the Boyds family since 1992, the majority of the piggish pieces were not offered until much later. About half the pigs released into the pen are still hanging out at the water trough, though, including two which made their debut in 1999.

Aphrodite
7" • #5537 • AM
Issued: 1994 • Retired: 1995
Orig. Price: $12 • **Value: $43**

Aphrodite
7" • #5539 • AM
Issued: 1995 • Retired: 1996
Orig. Price: $12 • **Value: $43**

Erin O'Pigg
11" • #5536-09 • AM
Issued: 1996 • Retired: 1997
Orig. Price: $14 • **Value: $30**

Farland O'Pigg
16" • #5538 • AM
Issued: 1992 • Retired: 1997
Orig. Price: $29 • **Value: $56**

PIGS

	Price Paid	Value Of My Collection
1.		
2.		
3.		
4.		
5.		
6.		
7.		

PENCIL TOTALS

New!

Kaitlin K. Trufflesnout
8" • #91601-03 • TJ
Issued: 1999 • Current
Orig. Price: $12 • **Value: $12**

Kaitlin McSwine
8" • #91601 • TJ
Issued: 1997 • To Be Retired: 1999
Orig. Price: $12 • **Value: $12**

Kaitlin McSwine II
8" • #91601-01 • TJ
Issued: 1997 • Current
Orig. Price: $14 • **Value: $14**

(1)

Kaitlin McSwine III
8" • #91601-02 • TJ
Issued: 1998 • Current
Orig. Price: $16 • **Value: $16**

(2)

Lofton Q. McSwine
8" • #55391-09 • AM
Issued: 1997 • Current
Orig. Price: $11 • **Value: $11**

(3)

Maggie O'Pigg
11" • #5536-07 • AM
Issued: 1993 • Current
Orig. Price: $14 • **Value: $14**

(4)

Primrose
11" • #9160 • TJ
Issued: 1993 • Retired: 1996
Orig. Price: $20 • **Value: $48**

(5)

Primrose II
11" • #9160-01 • TJ
Issued: 1997 • Retired: 1997
Orig. Price: $20 • **Value: $38**

(6)

Primrose III
11" • #9160-02 • TJ
Issued: 1998 • Current
Orig. Price: $23 • **Value: $23**

(7)
New!

Primrose P. Trufflesnout
11" • #9160-03 • TJ
Issued: 1999 • Current
Orig. Price: $23 • **Value: $23**

(8)

Reilly O'Pigg
16" • #5538-07 • AM
Issued: 1993 • Retired: 1995
Orig. Price: $29 • **Value: $70**

(9)

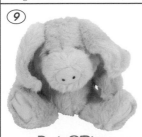

Rosie O'Pigg
11" • #5536 • AM
Issued: 1992 • Retired: 1998
Orig. Price: $14 • **Value: $28**

(10)

Sheffield O'Swine
8" • #55391-07 • AM
Issued: 1997 • Current
Orig. Price: $11 • **Value: $11**

PIGS (side tab)

	Price Paid	Value Of My Collection
1.		
2.		
3.		
4.		
5.		
6.		
7.		
8.		
9.		
10.		
PENCIL TOTALS		

ORNAMENTS

With 60 ornaments ranging from antique dolls to flying pigs, these pieces have become more than just Christmas decorations. The 1999 debut of two angel bears, two angel hares and two bears in bee costumes, along with 32 other current pieces, make these ornaments perfect for any season.

Angelica
7" • #5611-08 • OR
Issued: 1993 • Retired: 1997
Orig. Price: $12 • **Value: $20**

Angelina
5.5" • #5615-07 • OR
Issued: 1995 • Retired: 1997
Orig. Price: $7 • **Value: $15**

Angelina II
5.5" • #56151-07 • OR
Issued: 1998 • Current
Orig. Price: $7 • **Value: $7**

Ariel
5" • #5620-08 • OR
Issued: 1995 • Current
Orig. Price: $7 • **Value: $7**

ORNAMENTS

	Price Paid	Value Of My Collection
1.		
2.		
3.		
4.		
5.		
6.		
7.		
8.		
PENCIL TOTALS		

Arinna Goodnight
5.5" • #56231-04 • OR
Issued: 1997 • Current
Orig. Price: $7 • **Value: $7**

Athena
5.5" • #5617-01 • OR
Issued: 1995 • Retired: 1996
Orig. Price: $7 • **Value: $29**

New!

Aurora Goodnight
5.5" • #56232-12 • OR
Issued: 1999 • Current
Orig. Price: $7 • **Value: $7**

New!

Bibi Buzzby
5.5" • #56220-12 • OR
Issued: 1999 • Current
Orig. Price: $8 • **Value: $8**

①

Billy Bob
5" • #56201-06 • OR
Issued: 1997 • Current
Orig. Price: $7 • **Value: $7**

② New!

Bud Buzzby
5.5" • #56220-08 • OR
Issued: 1999 • Current
Orig. Price: $8 • **Value: $8**

③

Cassie Goodnight
5.5" • #56232-01 • OR
Issued: 1998 • Current
Orig. Price: $7 • **Value: $7**

④

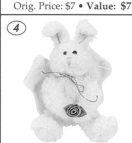

Celeste
5" • #5609-01 • OR
Issued: 1994 • To Be Retired: 1999
Orig. Price: $7 • **Value: $7**

⑤

Celestina Goodnight
5.5" • #56231-02 • OR
Issued: 1997 • Current
Orig. Price: $7 • **Value: $7**

⑥

Clarence
4.5" • #5608-08 • OR
Issued: 1993 • Retired: 1996
Orig. Price: $6 • **Value: $24**

⑦

Comet
5.5" • #5622 • OR
Issued: 1996 • Current
Orig. Price: $7 • **Value: $7**

⑧

Corona Goodspeed
5.5" • #5624-09 • OR
Issued: 1998 • Current
Orig. Price: $7 • **Value: $7**

⑨

Country Angel
4.5" • #7401 • OR
Issued: 1993 • Retired: 1993
Orig. Price: N/A • **Value: $34**

⑩

Cowsies
5" • #5607 • OR
Issued: 1993 • Retired: 1994
Orig. Price: $5 • **Value: $45**

ORNAMENTS

	Price Paid	Value Of My Collection
1.		
2.		
3.		
4.		
5.		
6.		
7.		
8.		
9.		
10.		

✏ **PENCIL TOTALS**

ORNAMENTS

①

Deitrich
5.5" • #5608-06 • OR
Issued: 1996 • Retired: 1997
Orig. Price: $6 • **Value: $15**

②

Dipper
7" • #5611-09 • OR
Issued: 1996 • Retired: 1998
Orig. Price: $12 • **Value: $16**

③ New!

Echo Goodnight
5.5" • #56232-14 • OR
Issued: 1999 • Current
Orig. Price: $7 • **Value: $7**

④

Edna May
5" • #56201-02 • OR
Issued: 1997 • Current
Orig. Price: $7 • **Value: $7**

⑤

Gabriella
8" • #7408 • OR
Issued: 1994 • Retired: 1995
Orig. Price: $8 • **Value: N/E**

⑥

Gabriella
8" • #7408-08 • OR
Issued: 1996 • Retired: 1997
Orig. Price: $8 • **Value: N/E**

ORNAMENTS

	Price Paid	Value Of My Collection
1.		
2.		
3.		
4.		
5.		
6.		
7.		
8.		
9.		
10.		

✎ PENCIL TOTALS

⑦

Galaxy
7" • #56111-01 • OR
Issued: 1998 • Current
Orig. Price: $12 • **Value: $12**

⑧

Gweneth
5" • #56031 • OR
Issued: 1997 • To Be Retired: 1999
Orig. Price: $6 • **Value: $6**

⑨

Immanuella
5" • #5609-09 • OR
Issued: 1996 • To Be Retired: 1999
Orig. Price: $7 • **Value: $7**

⑩

Juliette
4.5" • #5612-01 • OR
Issued: 1994 • Current
Orig. Price: $7 • **Value: $7**

①

Jupiter Goodspeed
5.5" • #5624-06 • OR
Issued: 1998 • Current
Orig. Price: $7 • **Value: $7**

②

Lambsies
4.5" • #5603 • OR
Issued: 1991 • Retired: 1995
Orig. Price: $5 • **Value: $28**

③

Linnea
7" • #5610-01 • OR
Issued: 1994 • Retired: 1997
Orig. Price: $12 • **Value: $20**

④

Lionsies
4.5" • #5604 • OR
Issued: 1991 • Retired: 1994
Orig. Price: $5 • **Value: $55**

⑤

Lorelei
5.5" • #56141 • OR
Issued: 1997 • Current
Orig. Price: $7 • **Value: $7**

⑥

Luna
5" • #5621-10 • OR
Issued: 1996 • Retired: 1997
Orig. Price: $6 • **Value: $13**

⑦

Matilda
5.5" • #5617-05 • OR
Issued: 1995 • Current
Orig. Price: $7 • **Value: $7**

⑧

Mercer
5.5" • #56171-03 • OR
Issued: 1998 • Current
Orig. Price: $7 • **Value: $7**

⑨

Mercury
7" • #5610-09 • OR
Issued: 1996 • Retired: 1998
Orig. Price: $12 • **Value: $17**

⑩
New!

Moondust Goodspeed
5.5" • #5624-08 • OR
Issued: 1999 • Current
Orig. Price: $7 • **Value: $7**

ORNAMENTS

	Price Paid	Value Of My Collection
1.		
2.		
3.		
4.		
5.		
6.		
7.		
8.		
9.		
10.		
	PENCIL TOTALS	

ORNAMENTS

**① **

Moosies
6" • #5605 • OR
Issued: 1993 • Retired: 1996
Orig. Price: $5 • **Value: $27**

**② **

Narcissus
5" • #5621-08 • OR
Issued: 1996 • Retired: 1997
Orig. Price: $6 • **Value: $13**

**③ **

Orion
5" • #5612-09 • OR
Issued: 1996 • Current
Orig. Price: $7 • **Value: $7**

**④ **

Ovid
4.5" • #5614 • OR
Issued: 1994 • Retired: 1996
Orig. Price: $7 • **Value: $24**

**⑤ **

Pair O'Bears
info unavailable
Orig. Price: N/A • **Value: N/E**

**⑥ **

Pair O'Bears
4.5" • #5601 • OR
Issued: pre-1990 • Retired: 1996
Orig. Price: $5 • **Value: $48**

ORNAMENTS

	Price Paid	Value Of My Collection
1.		
2.		
3.		
4.		
5.		
6.		
7.		
8.		
9.		

✏ PENCIL TOTALS

**⑦ **

Pair O'Hares
6" • #5600 • OR
Issued: 1991 • Retired: 1994
Orig. Price: $5 • **Value: $44**

**⑧ **

Pair O'Hares
6" • #5602 • OR
Issued: 1990 • Retired: 1991
Orig. Price: $5 • **Value: N/E**

**⑨ **

Pair O'Highland Plaid Bear
5" • #5618-02 • OR
Issued: 1996 • Retired: 1998
Orig. Price: $4 • **Value: $7**

①

Pair O'Homespun Bears
5" • #5618 • OR
Issued: 1995 • Retired: 1996
Orig. Price: $4 • **Value: $35**

②

Pair O'Piggs
6" • #5606 • OR
Issued: 1993 • Retired: 1996
Orig. Price: $5 • **Value: $50**

③

Raggedy Twins
4.5" • #7400 • OR
Issued: 1993 • Retired: 1995
Orig. Price: $6 • **Value: $80**

④

Regulus P. Roar
5" • #56041 • OR
Issued: 1997 • Current
Orig. Price: $6 • **Value: $6**

⑤

Seraphina
5" • #5615 • OR
Issued: 1994 • Current
Orig. Price: $7 • **Value: $7**

⑥

Serena Goodnight
5.5" • #56232-08 • OR
Issued: 1998 • Current
Orig. Price: $7 • **Value: $7**

⑦

Silverton Snowbeary
5" • #56191 • OR
Issued: 1998 • Current
Orig. Price: $7 • **Value: $7**

⑧

New!

Stardust Goodspeed
5.5" • #5624-01 • OR
Issued: 1999 • Current
Orig. Price: $7 • **Value: $7**

⑨

Stella Goodnight
5.5" • #5623-09 • OR
Issued: 1997 • Current
Orig. Price: $7 • **Value: $7**

⑩

Venus
4.5" • #5616 • OR
Issued: 1994 • Retired: 1996
Orig. Price: $7 • **Value: $27**

ORNAMENTS

	Price Paid	Value Of My Collection
1.		
2.		
3.		
4.		
5.		
6.		
7.		
8.		
9.		
10.		

✏ PENCIL TOTALS

ORNAMENTS

①
White Snowberry Bear
5" • #5619 • OR
Issued: 1995 • Retired: 1996
Orig. Price: $7 • **Value: N/E**

②
Willie S. Hydrant IV
5.5" • #5625 • OR
Issued: 1998 • Current
Orig. Price: $7 • **Value: $7**

③
Zephyr Goodnight
5.5" • #5623-06 • OR
Issued: 1997 • Current
Orig. Price: $7 • **Value: $7**

COLLECTOR'S CLUB

In 1996, The Loyal Order of Friends of Boyds kicked off its charter year. Since then, members have enjoyed a multitude of benefits, including 16 exclusive pieces.

④ New!
Bloomin' F.o.B.
pin • #01999-11 • F.o.B.
Issued: 1999 • To Be Retired: 1999
Membership Gift • **Value: N/E**

⑤ New!
Blossom B. Berriweather ...Bloom With Joy!
N/A • #01999-21 • F.o.B.
Issued: 1999 • To Be Retired: 1999
Membership Gift • **Value: N/E**

ORNAMENTS

	Price Paid	Value Of My Collection
1.		
2.		
3.		

COLLECTOR'S CLUB

4.		
5.		
6.		
7.		
8.		
9.		

PENCIL TOTALS

⑥
Eleanor
6" • #01998-31 • F.o.B.
Issued: 1998 • Retired: 1998
Membership Gift • **Value: N/E**

⑦ New!
Flora Mae Berriweather
6" • #01999-31 • F.o.B.
Issued: 1999 • To Be Retired: 1999
Membership Gift • **Value: N/E**

⑧
Lady Liberty
pin • #01998-11 • F.o.B.
Issued: 1998 • Retired: 1998
Membership Gift • **Value: N/E**

⑨
Lady Liberty
N/A • #01998-21 • F.o.B.
Issued: 1998 • Retired: 1998
Membership Gift • **Value: N/E**

①

Ms. Berriweather's Cottage
N/A • #01998-41 • F.o.B.
Issued: 1998 • Retired: 1998
Orig. Price: $21 • **Value: N/E**

② New!

Noah's Genius At Work Table
Noah's Pageant Series
N/A • #2429 • F.o.B.
Issued: 1999 • To Be Retired: 1999
Orig. Price: $11.50 • **Value: $11.50**

③ New!

Plant With Hope, Grow With Love, Bloom With Joy
6" & 6" & 6" • #01999-51 • F.o.B.
Issued: 1999 • To Be Retired: 1999
Orig. Price: $25 • **Value: $25**

④

Raeburn
6" • #01996-31 • F.o.B.
Issued: 1996 • Retired: 1997
Membership Gift • **Value: $30**

⑤ New!

Sunny And Sally Berriweather ... Plant With Hope
N/A • #01999-41 • F.o.B.
Issued: 1999 • To Be Retired: 1999
Orig. Price: $23 • **Value: $23**

⑥

Uncle Elliot
pin • #01996-11 • F.o.B.
Issued: 1996 • Retired: 1997
Membership Gift • **Value: $22**

⑦

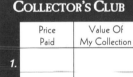

Uncle Elliot ... The Head Bean Wants You
N/A • #01996-21 • F.o.B.
Issued: 1996 • Retired: 1997
Membership Gift • **Value: $80**

⑧

Velma Q. Berriweather
11" • #01996-51 • F.o.B.
Issued: 1997 • Retired: 1997
Orig. Price: $29 • **Value: $60**

⑨

Velma Q. Berriweather ... The Cookie Queen
N/A • #01996-41 • F.o.B.
Issued: 1997 • Retired: 1997
Orig. Price: $19 • **Value: $67**

⑩

Zelma G. Berriweather
11" • #01998-51 • F.o.B.
Issued: 1998 • Retired: 1998
Orig. Price: $32 • **Value: N/E**

COLLECTOR'S CLUB

	Price Paid	Value Of My Collection
1.		
2.		
3.		
4.		
5.		
6.		
7.		
8.		
9.		
10.		

✏ **PENCIL TOTALS**

BOYDS PLUSH EXCLUSIVES

Exclusive pieces, or those that are made available in limited numbers and offered through selected outlets, have been produced for a number of businesses, from retail stores to catalogs. Some of these pieces, especially the ones on QVC, are launches or early releases, meaning that they will appear later in the regular line. However most of them are exclusives and often become unavailable before most collectors even have the chance to discover them. As a result, not only are these critters elusive, so is their relevant information.

EXCLUSIVE BEARS

Because bears are the most popular characters in the Boyds line, several outlets have taken the opportunity to offer specially designed Boyds pieces as exclusives. In the past five years, over 300 exclusive bears have clawed their way into the collection.

①

Aberdeen
QVC
Issued: 1994
Value: N/E

②

Abigail
Bon-Ton
Issued: 1996
Value: N/E

BEARS
— EXCLUSIVE —

	Price Paid	Value Of My Collection
1.		
2.		
3.		
4.		
5.		
6.		
7.		
8.		

PENCIL TOTALS

③

Abigail
Elder-Beerman
Issued: 1998
Value: N/E

④

Adkin
Frederick Atkins
10"
Issued: 1997
Value: $26

⑤

Al'Berta B. Bear
(LE-10,000)
Canadian
10" • #BC94277
Issued: 1998
Value: $37

⑥

Aldina
Dillard's
#94714DL
Issued: 1997
Value: $45

⑦
New!

Alex Nicole
Dillard's
10" • #94743DL
Issued: 1999
Value: $18

⑧

Alexis Bearinsky
GCC
16" • #94862GCC
Issued: 1998
Value: $46

① 	② 	③ New! PHOTO UNAVAILABLE	④ 
Ally *Lord & Taylor* 8" Issued: 1997 **Value: $26**	**Anastasia** *QVC* Issued: 1995 **Value: $80**	**Andrew** *Dillard's* 10" • #94742DL Issued: 1999 **Value: $18**	**Angeline** *QVC* Issued: 1997 **Value: N/E**

⑤ 	⑥ 	⑦ PHOTO UNAVAILABLE 	⑧ PHOTO UNAVAILABLE
Annabella *GCC (Early Release)* 12" • #912072GCC Issued: 1998 **Value: $30**	**Annabelle Z. Witebred** *QVC* Issued: 1998 **Value: $34**	**Arlo** *Select Retailers* *info unavailable* **Value: N/E**	**Artemus J. Bear** *Country Living* 16" Issued: 1997 **Value: $45**

⑨ 	⑩ 	⑪ 
Artie Finkmorton, Izzy Wingnut & Norton Flapjack *QVC* Issued: 1998 **Value: N/E**	**Attie** *Frederick Atkins* 8" Issued: 1997 **Value: $40**	**Aubrey** *Dillard's* 14" • #94723DL Issued: 1997 **Value: $40**

⑫ 	⑬ New! 	⑭
Aubrey *GCC* 10" • #94863GCC Issued: 1998 **Value: $35**	**Aunt Becky Bearchild** *The San Francisco Music Box Company* ♪ *Whistle While You Work* 12" • #912052SF Issued: 1999 **Value: $35**	**Aunt Phiddy Bearburn** *JT Webb* Issued: 1998 **Value: N/E**

BEARS
— EXCLUSIVE —

	Price Paid	Value Of My Collection
1.		
2.		
3.		
4.		
5.		
6.		
7.		
8.		
9.		
10.		
11.		
12.		
13.		
14.		

✏ PENCIL TOTALS

EXCLUSIVE BEARS

①

Auntie Adeline
*Carson Pirie
Scott & Co.*
10"
Issued: 1997
Value: $50

②

**Auntie Edna,
Flora & Tillie**
QVC
Issued: 1998
Value: N/E

③

**Auntie Esther &
Theona DoLittle
(LE-1,800)**
QVC
Issued: 1998
Value: N/E

④

Bailey (Spring 1996)
QVC
8" • TJ
Issued: 1996
Value: $200

⑤

Bailey (Spring 1997)
QVC
8" • TJ
Issued: 1997
Value: N/E

⑥

Bailey (Spring 1998)
QVC
8" • TJ
Issued: 1998
Value: N/E

⑦

Barnard B. Bear
Barnes & Noble
10"
Issued: 1998
Value: $38

⑧

Barney B. Keeper
Bon-Ton
Issued: 1997
Value: N/E

BEARS
— EXCLUSIVE —

	Price Paid	Value Of My Collection
1.		
2.		
3.		
4.		
5.		
6.		
7.		
8.		
9.		
10.		
11.		
12.		
13.		
14.		

 PENCIL TOTALS

⑨

Barret
Select Retailers
Issued: 1996
Value: $72

⑩

Barston Q. Growler
QVC
Issued: 1997
Value: $42

⑪

**Bath & Body
Works Bear**
Bath & Body Works
Issued: 1996
Value: N/E

⑫

Bauer B. Bear
Eddie Bauer
12"
Issued: 1998
Value: N/E

⑬

Beatrice
Elder-Beerman
10"
Issued: 1998
Value: N/E

⑭

Beauregard
QVC
info unavailable
Value: $45

(1)

Beauregard
Select Retailers
Issued: 1996
Value: N/E

(2)

Belk Bear
Belk
Issued: 1997
Value: N/E

(3)

Benjamin Beanbeary
Belk
8"
Issued: 1998
Value: N/E

(4)

Benjamin Bear
*The San Francisco
Music Box Company*
♪ *Let Me Be Your Teddy Bear*
12" • #41-72142
Issued: 1998
Value: $36

(5)

PHOTO UNAVAILABLE

Berret
Select Retailers
8"
Issued: 1996
Value: N/E

(6)

Betty Lou
QVC
Issued: 1996
Value: $270

(7)

Bill
QVC
Issued: 1995
Value: N/E

(8)

Bingham
QVC
22"
Issued: 1998
Value: N/E

(9)

Blackstone
QVC
Issued: 1997
Value: N/E

(10)

Boo B. Bear
QVC
Issued: 1997
Value: N/E

(11)

PHOTO UNAVAILABLE

Boo Bear
Marshall Field's
Issued: 1994
Value: N/E

(12)

Boo-Boo
Select Retailers
Issued: 1998
Value: $29

(13)

Bosley & Chadwick
QVC
Issued: 1997
Value: N/E

BEARS	
— EXCLUSIVE —	
Price Paid	Value Of My Collection
1.	
2.	
3.	
4.	
5.	
6.	
7.	
8.	
9.	
10.	
11.	
12.	
13.	
✏ PENCIL TOTALS	

EXCLUSIVE BEARS

①

Brandie & Madeira
QVC
Issued: 1998
Value: N/E

②

Brandon
Dillard's
#94703DL
Issued: 1996
Value: $26

③

Braxton
*The San Francisco
Music Box Company*
♪ *I Will Always Love You*
14" • #41-72640
Issued: 1998
Value: N/E

④

Bria
Select Retailers
Issued: 1998
Value: N/E

⑤

Brian
Canadian
12" • #BC100708 • PM
Issued: 1997
Value: $30

⑥

PHOTO
UNAVAILABLE

Brianne
Frederick Atkins
10"
Issued: 1998
Value: N/E

⑦

**Brighton, Salisbury &
Somerset**
QVC
Issued: 1998
Value: N/E

⑧

Bronson
Select Retailers
Issued: 1996
Value: $30

⑨

Brumley
QVC
Issued: 1997
Value: $30

⑩

Bruno Bedlington
QVC
Issued: 1998
Value: N/E

⑪

Buchanan J. Bearington
QVC
11"
Issued: 1998
Value: N/E

⑫

PHOTO
UNAVAILABLE

Buckles
Lord & Taylor
Issued: 1997
Value: N/E

⑬

Buffy
Victoria's Secret
Issued: 1996
Value: $40

⑭

Buford B.
QVC
Issued: 1997
Value: $48

(1)

Burgess P. Bear
QVC
info unavailable
Value: N/E

(2)

PHOTO
UNAVAILABLE

Burt
Select Retailers
info unavailable
Value: N/E

(3)

C. Elbert
Dillard's
17" • #94720DL
Issued: 1997
Value: $45

(4)

PHOTO
UNAVAILABLE

**Caledonia,
Humboldt & Shasta**
QVC
Issued: 1998
Value: N/E

(5)

Caroline
QVC
Issued: 1996
Value: $50

(6)

Casimir B. Bean
GCC
#94858GCC
Issued: 1998
Value: $38

(7)

Cass
Select Retailers
Issued: 1998
Value: N/E

(8)

Cassidy
QVC
Issued: 1997
Value: $80

(9)

Ceylon Pekoe
QVC
Issued: 1997
Value: $55

(10)

Chamomille
*The San Francisco
Music Box Company*
♪ A Dream Is A Wish Your
Heart Makes
11" • #41-72645
Issued: 1998
Value: N/E

(11)

Chandler
Select Retailers
8"
Issued: 1997
Value: $33

(12)

Christmas Bear
QVC
Issued: 1995
Value: $165

(13)

Cimmaron
QVC
Issued: 1997
Value: N/E

(14)

Clara
Bon-Ton
14"
Issued: 1996
Value: N/E

BEARS
— EXCLUSIVE —

	Price Paid	Value Of My Collection
1.		
2.		
3.		
4.		
5.		
6.		
7.		
8.		
9.		
10.		
11.		
12.		
13.		
14.		

✏ PENCIL TOTALS

EXCLUSIVE BEARS

①  **Clara** *Kirlin's* Issued: 1996 **Value: $42**	②  **Clarissa** *The San Francisco Music Box Company* ♪ *Make Someone Happy* 15" • #41-72584 Issued: 1998 **Value: N/E**	③ **Clark** *QVC* 10" Issued: 1998 **Value: N/E**	④  **Claudette** *Country Gift* *info unavailable* **Value: N/E**
⑤  **Claudius B. Bean** *Lord & Taylor* 14" Issued: 1998 **Value: N/E**	⑥  **Claudius B. Bean** *QVC* Issued: 1997 **Value: $50**	⑦  **Clementine** *Elder-Beerman* 14" Issued: 1997 **Value: N/E**	⑧  **Colleen** *QVC* *info unavailable* **Value: N/E**

BEARS
— EXCLUSIVE —

	Price Paid	Value Of My Collection
1.		
2.		
3.		
4.		
5.		
6.		
7.		
8.		
9.		
10.		
11.		
12.		
13.		

✏ **PENCIL TOTALS**

⑨  **Collette** *Select Retailers* Issued: 1997 **Value: N/E**	⑩ **Corliss & Quincy** *QVC* 8" & 8" Issued: 1998 **Value: N/E**	⑪ PHOTO UNAVAILABLE **Cosmos** *Elder-Beerman* Issued: 1998 **Value: N/E**
⑫  **Courtney** *QVC* 16" Issued: 1998 **Value: $45**	⑬  **Cranston** *GCC* 8.25" • #94855GCC Issued: 1997 **Value: $32**	

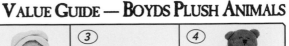

1

Cromwell
QVC
Issued: 1997
Value: N/E

2

Danielle &
Elizabieta de Bearvoire
QVC
Issued: 1997
Value: N/E

3

Darby
Select Retailers
Issued: 1997
Value: N/E

4

Daria & Dickens
QVC
8" & 8"
Issued: 1998
Value: N/E

5

Dean B. Bearberg
Select Retailers
info unavailable
Value: N/E

6
New!

PHOTO
UNAVAILABLE

Debbie Claire
Dillard's
12" • #94741DL
Issued: 1999
Value: $35

7

Deidre Rose
Bon-Ton
12"
Issued: 1997
Value: $44

8

Delilah & Twila
Higgenthorpe
QVC
Issued: 1998
Value: N/E

9

Delmarva V.
Crackenpot
QVC
Issued. 1997
Value: N/E

10

Dessa & Rochelle
QVC
Issued: 1998
Value: N/E

11

Dion Bearberg
Select Retailers
Issued: 1998
Value: $32

12

Douglas
Select Retailers
Issued: 1996
Value: N/E

13

Duncan
Select Retailers
info unavailable
Value: N/E

14

Eddie Bauer Diamond
Eddie Bauer
Issued: 1997
Value: $45

BEARS
— EXCLUSIVE —

	Price Paid	Value Of My Collection
1.		
2.		
3.		
4.		
5.		
6.		
7.		
8.		
9.		
10.		
11.		
12.		
13.		
14.		

PENCIL TOTALS

EXCLUSIVE BEARS

①

Eddie Bauer Hunter
Eddie Bauer
Issued: 1996
Value: $70

②

Edmund
Eddie Bauer
Issued: 1994
Value: $125

③

PHOTO UNAVAILABLE

Edwin R. Elfstein
Lord & Taylor
Issued: 1996
Value: N/E

④

Effie May
Bon-Ton
12" • AS
Issued: 1998
Value: N/E

⑤

Elisia P. Bearypoppin, Darrell & Ross
QVC
Issued: 1997
Value: N/E

⑥

Ella
Dillard's
8" • #94724DL
Issued: 1997
Value: $37

⑦

Elliot
Select Retailers
info unavailable
Value: N/E

⑧

PHOTO UNAVAILABLE

Elmore Elf Bear
QVC
Issued: 1996
Value: $36

BEARS
— EXCLUSIVE —

	Price Paid	Value Of My Collection
1.		
2.		
3.		
4.		
5.		
6.		
7.		
8.		
9.		
10.		
11.		
12.		
13.		

✏ PENCIL TOTALS

⑨

Elsbeth
Dillard's
#94704DL
Issued: 1996
Value: N/E

⑩

Elton
QVC
Issued: 1996
Value: $73

⑪

Emily Claire
Welcome Home
Issued: 1998
Value: $44

⑫

Emma
Elder-Beerman
Issued: 1998
Value: $42

⑬

Englebert Q. Elfberg
GCC
10" • #94857GCC
Issued: 1998
Value: $34

1

Erin
Lord & Taylor
Issued: 1997
Value: $26

2

PHOTO UNAVAILABLE

Eugenia
Dillard's
Issued: 1997
Value: $75

3

Eugenia
The San Francisco Music Box Company
♪ *Can't Help Falling In Love*
16" • #56-66601
Issued: 1997
Value: N/E

4

Evan & Sheldon Bearchild
QVC
5.5" & 5.5"
Issued: 1998
Value: N/E

5

PHOTO UNAVAILABLE

Eve
Select Retailers
info unavailable
Value: N/E

6

Ewell Manitoba Mooselman (LE-2,400)
Canadian
#BC94275
Issued: 1997
Value: $55

7

Felicity
Lord & Taylor
Issued: 1997
Value: $20

8

Fidelity
The San Francisco Music Box Company
♪ *Love Will Keep Us Together*
17" • #41-72638
Issued: 1998
Value: N/E

9

Fillmore
QVC
Issued: 1998
Value: N/E

10

Francesca
Bon-Ton
14"
Issued: 1998
Value: N/E

11

Frankie Bearberg
Select Retailers
Issued: 1998
Value: $32

12

Fredrica
Select Retailers
Issued: 1997
Value: N/E

13

Gabriella
Parade Of Gifts
6" • #94579POG
Issued: 1998
Value: $20

14

PHOTO UNAVAILABLE

Gareth & Glynnis
QVC
8" & 8"
Issued: 1998
Value: N/E

BEARS
— EXCLUSIVE —

	Price Paid	Value Of My Collection
1.		
2.		
3.		
4.		
5.		
6.		
7.		
8.		
9.		
10.		
11.		
12.		
13.		
14.		

PENCIL TOTALS

EXCLUSIVE BEARS

① 	② 	③ 	④ 
Gatsby *Bon-Ton* 12" Issued: 1998 Value: N/E	**Geneva** *Select Retailers* Issued: 1996 Value: $40	**George** *May Department Store Company* 6" Issued: 1998 Value: N/E	**George** *QVC* Issued: 1996 Value: N/E
⑤ 	⑥ 	⑦	⑧ 
Geraldine & Sylvester *QVC* Issued: 1998 Value: N/E	**Gideon** *QVC* 10" Issued: 1998 Value: N/E	**Glenna** *Dillard's* 7" • #94721DL Issued: 1997 Value: $55	**Gracie** *May Department Store Company* 6" Issued: 1998 Value: N/E

<table>
<tr><td colspan="3">

BEARS
— *EXCLUSIVE* —
</td></tr>
<tr><td></td><td>Price Paid</td><td>Value Of My Collection</td></tr>
<tr><td>1.</td><td></td><td></td></tr>
<tr><td>2.</td><td></td><td></td></tr>
<tr><td>3.</td><td></td><td></td></tr>
<tr><td>4.</td><td></td><td></td></tr>
<tr><td>5.</td><td></td><td></td></tr>
<tr><td>6.</td><td></td><td></td></tr>
<tr><td>7.</td><td></td><td></td></tr>
<tr><td>8.</td><td></td><td></td></tr>
<tr><td>9.</td><td></td><td></td></tr>
<tr><td>10.</td><td></td><td></td></tr>
<tr><td>11.</td><td></td><td></td></tr>
<tr><td>12.</td><td></td><td></td></tr>
<tr><td>13.</td><td></td><td></td></tr>
<tr><td>14.</td><td></td><td></td></tr>
<tr><td colspan="3">✏ PENCIL TOTALS</td></tr>
</table>

⑨ **New!**

PHOTO UNAVAILABLE

Gracie Bear
Dillard's
6" • #94739DL
Issued: 1999
Value: $8

⑩

Grandma Henrietta & Lizzie
QVC
Issued: 1997
Value: $120

⑪

Grant S. Bearington
Norm Thompson
Issued: 1997
Value: $70

⑫

Guilford
GCC
6" • #94852GCC
Issued: 1997
Value: $38

⑬

Guinevere
Lord & Taylor
Issued: 1996
Value: N/E

⑭

Guinevere
QVC
11"
Issued: 1997
Value: N/E

①

Guinevere
The San Francisco
Music Box Company
♪ *La Vie En Rose*
11" • #41-72139
Issued: 1998
Value: N/E

②

Gunnar
Select Retailers
info unavailable
Value: N/E

③

Gunter
Dillard's
10" • #94722DL
Issued: 1997
Value: $25

④

Guthrie P. Mussy
QVC
Issued: 1997
Value: N/E

⑤

Harry
Lord & Taylor
8"
Issued: 1997
Value: N/E

⑥

Heathcliff
QVC
Issued: 1997
Value: N/E

⑦

Hedda
QVC
Issued: 1996
Value: $78

⑧

Henry
Dillard's
14" • #94726DL
Issued: 1997
Value: $50

⑨

Holly Bearberry
QVC
Issued: 1996
Value: $48

⑩

Honey B. Bear
Spiegel
Issued: 1994
Value: N/E

⑪

Honey B. Elfberg
Parade Of Gifts
14" • #94578POG
Issued: 1998
Value: N/E

⑫

Honey B. Mine
Parade Of Gifts
14" • #94576POG
Issued: 1998
Value: N/E

⑬

Honey Bee Bear
Faith Mountain
Company
Issued: 1995
Value: N/E

BEARS
– EXCLUSIVE –

	Price Paid	Value Of My Collection
1.		
2.		
3.		
4.		
5.		
6.		
7.		
8.		
9.		
10.		
11.		
12.		
13.		
PENCIL TOTALS		

EXCLUSIVE BEARS

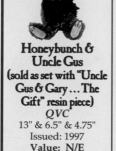

1

Honeybunch & Uncle Gus
(sold as set with "Uncle Gus & Gary … The Gift" resin piece)
QVC
13" & 6.5" & 4.75"
Issued: 1997
Value: N/E

2

Hubbard
QVC
Issued: 1996
Value: $50

3

Huett
QVC
Issued: 1997
Value: N/E

4

Huntley
QVC
Issued: 1997
Value: N/E

5

Ike D. Bearington
QVC
14"
Issued: 1998
Value: N/E

6

Indigo Jones
QVC
Issued: 1997
Value: $74

7

J.T. Jordan
Welcome Home
Issued: 1997
Value: N/E

8

Jackson
May Department Store Company
Issued: 1998
Value: N/E

BEARS
— EXCLUSIVE —

	Price Paid	Value Of My Collection
1.		
2.		
3.		
4.		
5.		
6.		
7.		
8.		
9.		
10.		
11.		
12.		
13.		
14.		

✏ PENCIL TOTALS

9

Jacqueline K. Bearington
QVC
Issued: 1998
Value: N/E

10

Jaime Lisa
Dillard's
Issued: 1998
Value: N/E

11

Jake
Dillard's
8"
Issued: 1998
Value: N/E

12

James & Malachi
QVC
Issued: 1998
Value: N/E

13

Jan B. Bearberg
Select Retailers
Issued: 1998
Value: N/E

14

Jarvis Boydsenberry
QVC
16"
Issued: 1998
Value: N/E

① JC Penney Bear
JC Penney
info unavailable
Value: N/E

② Jean
Canadian
14" • #BC100905 • PM
Issued: 1997
Value: N/E

③ Jeremiah
PHOTO UNAVAILABLE
Country Living
Issued: 1997
Value: N/E

④ Jeremy
Dillard's
14" • #94712DL
Issued: 1997
Value: $45

⑤ Jillian
Dillard's
16"
Issued: 1998
Value: N/E

⑥ Jobie & Kibby Bearington
QVC
Issued: 1998
Value: N/E

⑦ Joe
Canadian
10" • #BC100508 • PM
Issued: 1997
Value: N/E

⑧ John
Canadian
10" • #BC100505 • PM
Issued: 1997
Value: N/E

⑨ John William
QVC
Issued: 1997
Value: N/E

⑩ Jolee
May Department Store Company
Issued: 1998
Value: N/E

⑪ Joyelle
Ideation
Issued: 1998
Value: N/E

BEARS
— EXCLUSIVE —

	Price Paid	Value Of My Collection
1.		
2.		
3.		
4.		
5.		
6.		
7.		
8.		
9.		
10.		
11.		
12.		
13.		
14.		

PENCIL TOTALS

⑫ Julia
Dillard's
14" • #94719DL
Issued: 1997
Value: $60

⑬ Julian
Dillard's
info unavailable
Value: N/E

⑭ Jupiter
QVC
Issued: 1996
Value: $33

EXCLUSIVE BEARS

171

①	②	③	④

Justin
Dillard's
11" • #5106-11DL
Issued: 1997
Value: $32

Justina & Matthew
QVC
Issued: 1997
Value: $160

Karl Von Fuzzner
QVC
10"
Issued: 1998
Value: N/E

Kassandra Berrywinkle
QVC
12"
Issued: 1997
Value: $54

⑤	⑥	⑦	⑧

Kaufmann Bear
Kaufmann's
info unavailable
Value: N/E

Kelby
Frederick Atkins
14"
Issued: 1998
Value: N/E

Knut C. Berriman
QVC
8"
Issued: 1998
Value: N/E

Kris
Lord & Taylor
5"
Issued: 1997
Value: N/E

BEARS
— EXCLUSIVE —

	Price Paid	Value Of My Collection
1.		
2.		
3.		
4.		
5.		
6.		
7.		
8.		
9.		
10.		
11.		
12.		
13.		
14.		

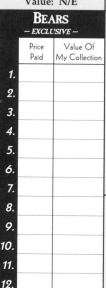

✏ **PENCIL TOTALS**

⑨	⑩	⑪

Kristoff
QVC
12"
Issued: 1998
Value: N/E

Kyle
Select Retailers
Issued: 1998
Value: $26

La Belle
Ideation
Issued: 1997
Value: N/E

⑫	⑬	⑭

Lara
QVC
Issued: 1997
Value: $140

Laura Ann
Dillard's
14"
Issued: 1998
Value: $47

Laura E. Bearburn (LE-5,000)
JT Webb
8"
Issued: 1997
Value: $40

① **PHOTO UNAVAILABLE** **Leo Bruinski** *QVC* *info unavailable* **Value: N/E**	②  **Leon** *Lord & Taylor* *info unavailable* **Value: N/E**	③ New!  **Leonardo B. Hartbreak** *QVC* 12" Issued: 1999 **Value: N/E**	④  **Lester** *Canadian* 12" • #BC100705 • PM Issued: 1997 **Value: N/E**
⑤  **Lewis** *QVC* Issued: 1998 **Value: N/E**	⑥  **Lindsey** *Belk* Issued: 1997 **Value: N/E**	⑦ New!  **Lindy & Nell Bradbeary** *QVC* 14" & 6" Issued: 1999 **Value: N/E**	⑧  **Linsey McKenzie** *QVC* Issued: 1997 **Value: $45**
⑨ **PHOTO UNAVAILABLE** **Little Larson** *Ideation* Issued: 1997 **Value: N/E**	⑩  **Liza Mae & Alex** *QVC* Issued: 1998 **Value: N/E**	⑪  **Lizzie McBee** *QVC* Issued: 1998 **Value: N/E**	
⑫  **Logan** *QVC* Issued: 1997 **Value: N/E**	⑬  **Lone Star** *Dillard's (Texas)* #94707DL Issued: 1996 **Value: $55**	⑭  **Lucinda D. Bearsley** *QVC* 10" Issued: 1998 **Value: N/E**	

BEARS
— EXCLUSIVE —

	Price Paid	Value Of My Collection
1.		
2.		
3.		
4.		
5.		
6.		
7.		
8.		
9.		
10.		
11.		
12.		
13.		
14.		

✏ PENCIL TOTALS

EXCLUSIVE BEARS

①  **Lucy Bea LeBruin** *QVC* Issued: 1997 Value: N/E	②  **Ludmilla Berriman & Ludwig Von Fuzzner (LE-2,400)** *QVC* 14" & 8" Issued: 1998 Value: N/E	③  **Madeline** *Elder-Beerman* 8" Issued: 1998 Value: N/E	④  **Madison** *Select Retailers* Issued: 1996 Value: N/E

⑤  **Magdalena** *Frederick Atkins* 6" Issued: 1998 Value: N/E	⑥ New! PHOTO UNAVAILABLE **Mallory Witebruin** *GCC* 14" • #94866GCC Issued: 1999 Value: N/E	⑦  **Mamie E. Bearington** *QVC* Issued: 1998 Value: N/E	⑧  **Margarita & Vermooth** *QVC* Issued: 1998 Value: N/E

BEARS
— EXCLUSIVE —

	Price Paid	Value Of My Collection
1.		
2.		
3.		
4.		
5.		
6.		
7.		
8.		
9.		
10.		
11.		
12.		
13.		
14.		

✏ PENCIL TOTALS

⑨  **Marian** *Kirlin's* 10" Issued: 1998 Value: N/E	⑩  **Marilyn** *Select Retailers* Issued: 1996 Value: $58	⑪  **Marina** *Lord & Taylor* 10" Issued: 1998 Value: N/E
⑫ PHOTO UNAVAILABLE **Marvelle** *Lord & Taylor* 11" Issued: 1997 Value: N/E	⑬ PHOTO UNAVAILABLE **Max** *Select Retailers* *info unavailable* Value: N/E	⑭  **Maximilian, Elford & Thornton** *QVC* 14" & 6" 3.5" Issued: 1998 Value: N/E

① 	② 	③ 	④ New! PHOTO UNAVAILABLE 
Maxton P. Bean *QVC* Issued: 1998 Value: N/E	**Michael** *Dillard's* 14" • #94717DL Issued: 1997 Value: $35	**Michaela** *Dillard's* 10" • #94718DL Issued: 1997 Value: $35	**Mindy Witebruin** *GCC* 6" • #94867GCC Issued: 1999 Value: N/E

⑤ 	⑥ 	⑦	⑧ 
Miss Isabelle Q. Bearworthy *QVC* 10" Issued: 1998 Value: N/E	**Momma Bear, Allouetta & Victor (LE-1,800)** *QVC* Issued: 1997 Value: $120	**Momma Berrywinkle & Woodrow (LE-2,400)** *QVC* 12" Issued: 1998 Value: $120	**Momma McBear & Cedric** *QVC* Issued: 1997 Value: $65

⑨	⑩ 	⑪ 	**BEARS** — *EXCLUSIVE* —
Momma McBear & Delmar *The San Francisco Music Box Company* ♪ *You're Nobody 'til Somebody Loves You* 10" & 6" • #41-72585 Issued: 1998 Value: N/E	**Momma McGoldberg & Cissy** *GCC* 10" • #94856GCC Issued: 1998 Value: $43	**Monica** *Frederick Atkins* 10" Issued: 1998 Value: $29	

	Price Paid	Value Of My Collection
1.		
2.		
3.		
4.		
5.		
6.		
7.		
8.		
9.		
10.		
11.		
12.		
13.		
14.		

⑫ 	⑬ 	⑭ 
Mother Bearston & Bluebell *QVC* Issued: 1998 Value: N/E	**Mr. BoJingles** *Select Retailers* Issued: 1997 Value: N/E	**Mrs. Bradley** *Linda Anderson's Collectibles* Issued: 1998 Value: N/E

PENCIL TOTALS

EXCLUSIVE BEARS

① 	②	③ 	④ 
Mrs. Potter & Amadeus (LE-1,200) *QVC* Issued: 1997 **Value: $140**	**Ms. Odetta & Neville** *QVC* Issued: 1996 **Value: $170**	**Nadia** *Kirlin's* 10" • AS Issued: 1998 **Value: N/E**	**Nadia Berriman** *QVC* 10" Issued: 1998 **Value: N/E**

⑤ PHOTO UNAVAILABLE	⑥ 	⑦ 	⑧ 
Nettie *QVC* Issued: 1994 **Value: N/E**	**Nichley** *Dillard's* Issued: 1998 **Value: $25**	**Nicholas, Ansel & Fitzgerald** *QVC* Issued: 1996 **Value: N/E**	**Nicholas & Nikki II** *Select Retailers* *info unavailable* **Value: N/E**

⑨ PHOTO UNAVAILABLE	⑩ 	⑪ 
Nicole *Dillard's* 8" Issued: 1998 **Value: N/E**	**Nicole de la El-bee** *Elder-Beerman* 14" Issued: 1997 **Value: $47**	**Niklas (LE-1,800)** *QVC* Issued: 1997 **Value: $150**

⑫ PHOTO UNAVAILABLE	⑬ 	⑭ PHOTO UNAVAILABLE
Noelle *Ethel M Chocolates* 6" Issued: 1998 **Value: N/E**	**Olas & Omar** *QVC* Issued: 1997 **Value: N/E**	**Oliver** *Dillard's* #94701DL Issued: 1996 **Value: N/E**

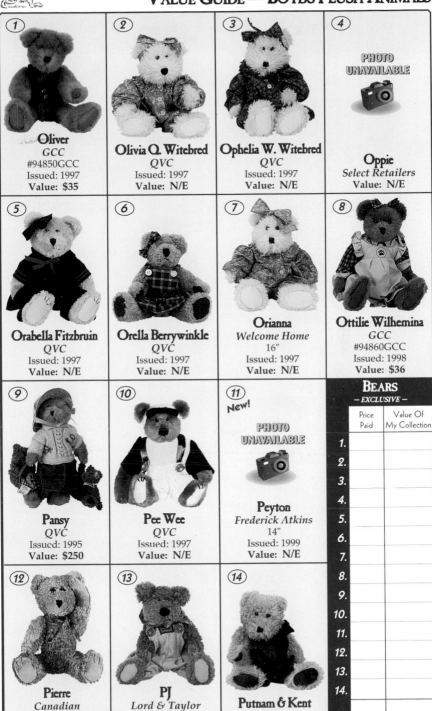

① Oliver
GCC
#94850GCC
Issued: 1997
Value: $35

② Olivia Q. Witebred
QVC
Issued: 1997
Value: N/E

③ Ophelia W. Witebred
QVC
Issued: 1997
Value: N/E

④
PHOTO UNAVAILABLE
Oppie
Select Retailers
Value: N/E

⑤ Orabella Fitzbruin
QVC
Issued: 1997
Value: N/E

⑥ Orella Berrywinkle
QVC
Issued: 1997
Value: N/E

⑦ Orianna
Welcome Home
16"
Issued: 1997
Value: N/E

⑧ Ottilie Wilhemina
GCC
#94860GCC
Issued: 1998
Value: $36

⑨ Pansy
QVC
Issued: 1995
Value: $250

⑩ Pee Wee
QVC
Issued: 1997
Value: N/E

⑪ New!
PHOTO UNAVAILABLE
Peyton
Frederick Atkins
14"
Issued: 1999
Value: N/E

⑫ Pierre
Canadian
14" • #BC100908 • PM
Issued: 1997
Value: $32

⑬ PJ
Lord & Taylor
8"
Issued: 1998
Value: N/E

⑭ Putnam & Kent
QVC
Issued: 1997
Value: $55

BEARS
— EXCLUSIVE —

	Price Paid	Value Of My Collection
1.		
2.		
3.		
4.		
5.		
6.		
7.		
8.		
9.		
10.		
11.		
12.		
13.		
14.		

✎ PENCIL TOTALS

EXCLUSIVE BEARS

① New! **PHOTO UNAVAILABLE** **Quinn** *Frederick Atkins* 16" Issued: 1999 Value: N/E	②  **Ragna** *Select Retailers* Issued: 1998 Value: $26	③  **Raylee** *Dillard's* 14" Issued: 1998 Value: $30	④  **Reba & Roxie DuBeary** *QVC* 6" & 6" Value: N/E
⑤  **Reginald** *Lord & Taylor* 16" Issued: 1996 Value: $60	⑥  **Remington B. Bean** *QVC* Issued: 1997 Value: N/E	⑦  **Rhoda** *GCC* #94854GCC Issued: 1997 Value: N/E	⑧  **Rodney** *Select Retailers* Issued: 1998 Value: $25

BEARS
— EXCLUSIVE —

	Price Paid	Value Of My Collection
1.		
2.		
3.		
4.		
5.		
6.		
7.		
8.		
9.		
10.		
11.		
12.		
13.		
14.		

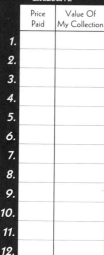

PENCIL TOTALS

⑨  **Roland** *Dillard's* 11" • #94725DL Issued: 1997 Value: $47	⑩  **Ronald** *Select Retailers* 8" Issued: 1997 Value: N/E	⑪  **Rosalind** *The San Francisco Music Box Company* ♪ Mr. Sandman 14" • #41-72125 Issued: 1997 Value: N/E
⑫ **Rosalind II** *The San Francisco Music Box Company* ♪ Mr. Sandman 14" • #41-72583 Issued: 1998 Value: N/E	⑬  **Rudolph** *Select Retailers* info unavailable Value: $30	⑭  **Rutledge** *QVC* Issued: 1998 Value: N/E

1

Samantha
Kirlin's
10"
Issued: 1997
Value: $37

2

Sarasota & Windsor
QVC
Issued: 1998
Value: N/E

3

Savannah Berrywinkle & Bentley
QVC
Issued: 1997
Value: $75

4

Scotch
Select Retailers
Issued: 1996
Value: N/E

5

Sedgewick T. Bruin
QVC
16"
Issued: 1998
Value: N/E

6

Sidney
Dillard's
10"
Issued: 1998
Value: N/E

7

Sissy
Lord & Taylor
8"
Issued: 1998
Value: N/E

8

Skylar & Starlynn
QVC
Issued: 1997
Value: N/E

9

Smith Witter II
The San Francisco Music Box Company
♪ *You've Got A Friend*
Issued: 1997
Value: $42

10

Stafford & Devon
GCC
8" • #94859GCC
Issued: 1998
Value: $56

11

Sterner
Frederick Atkins
10"
Issued: 1998
Value: $32

12

Sydney (LE-2,400)
Canadian
8" • #BC94276
Issued: 1997
Value: $46

13

T. Dean Newbearger
GCC
10" • #948656GCC
Issued: 1998
Value: N/E

14

Tammy
QVC
Issued: 1996
Value: $75

BEARS
— EXCLUSIVE —

	Price Paid	Value Of My Collection
1.		
2.		
3.		
4.		
5.		
6.		
7.		
8.		
9.		
10.		
11.		
12.		
13.		
14.		
	PENCIL TOTALS	

EXCLUSIVE BEARS

179

①

Tartan Tess
Country Peddler
Issued: 1996
Value: N/E

②

Taylor
Dillard's
16" • #94705DL
Issued: 1996
Value: $70

③

Ted & Teddy
QVC
Issued: 1994
Value: N/E

④

Teddy Bauer
QVC
Issued: 1995
Value: N/E

⑤

Texanne
Dillard's (Texas)
14" • #94708DL
Issued: 1996
Value: $60

⑥

**Thea St. Griz &
Everett Elfston**
QVC
17" & 7.5"
Issued: 1998
Value: N/E

⑦

Theodora Maria
QVC
Issued: 1998
Value: $53

⑧

**Thor & Katrinka
Berriman**
QVC
12" & 7"
Issued: 1998
Value: N/E

BEARS
— EXCLUSIVE —

	Price Paid	Value Of My Collection
1.		
2.		
3.		
4.		
5.		
6.		
7.		
8.		
9.		
10.		
11.		
12.		
13.		
14.		

✏ PENCIL TOTALS

⑨

Tillie
Select Retailers
Issued: 1998
Value: $37

⑩

Tyler
Dillard's
11"
Issued: 1998
Value: $52

⑪

**Uncle Zeb & Cousin
Minnow**
QVC
Issued: 1998
Value: N/E

⑫

Ursula Berriman
QVC
12"
Issued: 1998
Value: N/E

⑬

**Valentina, Caterina,
Evalina, & Michelina**
QVC
Issued: 1998
Value: $85

⑭

Venus
Elder-Beerman
Issued: 1998
Value: N/E

1

Verdeia
Frederick Atkins
16"
Issued: 1998
Value: N/E

2

Waitsfield
GCC
11" • #94853GCC
Issued: 1997
Value: $55

3

Walton
Canadian
Issued: 1997
Value: N/E

4

Wesley, Willoughby & Woodward
QVC
Issued: 1998
Value: $22

5

Will
Dillard's
6"
Issued: 1998
Value: N/E

6

Wilson (w/boat)
QVC
Issued: 1995
Value: N/E

7

PHOTO UNAVAILABLE
Wilson (w/pie)
QVC
Issued: 1994
Value: N/E

8

Winifred
Valentine's Day
Issued: 1997
Value: $35

9
New!

Winnie II
The San Francisco Music Box Company
♪ *Love Is Blue*
14"
Issued: 1999
Value: $35

10

Winstead & Pensacola
QVC
15" & 6"
Issued: 1998
Value: N/E

11

PHOTO UNAVAILABLE
Yolanda Panda
QVC
Issued: 1998
Value: N/E

12

Younker Bear
Younkers
info unavailable
Value: N/E

13

Yu'Kon B. Bear (LE-10,000)
Canadian
10" • #BC94278
Issued: 1998
Value: $35

14

Yvonne & Yvette
QVC
Issued: 1998
Value: N/E

BEARS
— EXCLUSIVE —

	Price Paid	Value Of My Collection
1.		
2.		
3.		
4.		
5.		
6.		
7.		
8.		
9.		
10.		
11.		
12.		
13.		
14.		

 PENCIL TOTALS

EXCLUSIVE BEARS

EXCLUSIVE CATS

The home shopping network QVC was the predominant dealer of exclusive Boyds cats until 1998. Since then, The San Francisco Music Box Company, Dillard's, Lord & Taylor and a few select retailers have joined in to offer several friendly feline exclusives.

1

Allie Fuzzbucket & Mugsy Tirebiter
QVC
9" & 9"
Issued: 1998
Value: N/E

2

Caleigh
Dillard's
11"
Issued: 1998
Value: N/E

3

Cher S. Fussberg
Select Retailers
Issued: 1998
Value: N/E

4

Claudia & Rowena Pussytoes
QVC
Issued: 1997
Value: $50

5

Cleo P. Pussytoes
QVC
Issued: 1997
Value: $55

6

Cleo P. Pussytoes
The San Francisco Music Box Company
♪ *What's New Pussycat?*
16" • #41-72140
Issued: 1998
Value: N/E

CATS
— EXCLUSIVE —

	Price Paid	Value Of My Collection
1.		
2.		
3.		
4.		
5.		
6.		
7.		
8.		
9.		
10.		
11.		
12.		

✏ PENCIL TOTALS

7

Crackers & Roquefort
QVC
Issued: 1998
Value: $42

8

Grosvenor Catberg
QVC
Issued: 1997
Value: $55

9

Heranamous
The San Francisco Music Box Company
♪ *Ebony And Ivory*
17" • #41-72639
Issued: 1998
Value: N/E

10

Ivana Purrkins
QVC
11"
Value: $30

11

Katie Kat
Lord & Taylor
16"
Issued: 1998
Value: N/E

12

Leslie G. Catberg
Select Retailers
Issued: 1998
Value: N/E

①

**Lindsey II &
Tucker F. Wuzzie**
QVC
Issued: 1998
Value: N/E

②

**Lyndon B. & Mondale
W. Cattington**
QVC
Issued: 1998
Value: N/E

③

Mrs. Petrie
QVC
13"
Value: N/E

④

**Terence, Thad &
Thristan**
QVC
info unavailable
Value: N/E

⑤

Thomasina Purrkins
QVC
info unavailable
Value: N/E

⑥

Whitefurd Felinsky
QVC
12"
Value: N/E

⑦

Zoe R. Grimilkin
QVC
11"
Issued: 1997
Value: $42

EXCLUSIVE COWS

An "udderly" great exclusive set, Adelaide and her sister Aggie share the honor of being members of this tiny grouping. The two huggable heifers were sold on QVC in 1998.

⑧

Adelaide & Aggie
QVC
Issued: 1998
Value: $45

EXCLUSIVE DOGS

Of the several dogs that have been offered as exclusives, three have made their debut through guest spots on QVC. Additionaly, two have been offered through the retail store Lord & Taylor, with some of the other remaining pooches coming from Bath & Body Works and the Casual Living catalog.

⑨

**Ambrose P.
Hydrant III**
QVC
Issued: 1997
Value: N/E

CATS		
— *EXCLUSIVE* —		
	Price Paid	Value Of My Collection
1.		
2.		
3.		
4.		
5.		
6.		
7.		

COWS		
— *EXCLUSIVE* —		
8.		

DOGS		
— *EXCLUSIVE* —		
9.		

✏ PENCIL TOTALS

EXCLUSIVE CATS/COWS/DOGS

①

PHOTO UNAVAILABLE

Ambrose Q. Hydrant
Lord & Taylor
Issued: 1998
Value: N/E

②

Bath & Body Works Dog
Bath & Body Works
Issued: 1996
Value: $45

③

Buzz
Lord & Taylor
10"
Issued: 1997
Value: N/E

④

Caesar Q. & Cosmo G. Hydrant
QVC
10" & 10"
Issued: 1998
Value: N/E

⑤

Corky
QVC
Issued: 1998
Value: N/E

⑥
PHOTO UNAVAILABLE

Salty
Casual Living
Issued: 1995
Value: N/E

DOGS
— EXCLUSIVE —

	Price Paid	Value Of My Collection
1.		
2.		
3.		
4.		
5.		
6.		

FROGS
— EXCLUSIVE —

7.		

GORILLAS
— EXCLUSIVE —

8.		

✏ PENCIL TOTALS

EXCLUSIVE FROGS

Not many frogs have dared to hop into the Boyds exclusive category, but "Nikali Q. Ribbit," offered on QVC in 1997, is a great green addition.

⑦

Nikali Q. Ribbit
QVC
Issued: 1997
Value: N/E

EXCLUSIVE GORILLAS

The trio, "Jake, Jay & Jette Magilla," who were sold as a set on QVC in 1998, are part of the notorious Magilla clan offered in the regular line.

⑧

Jake, Jay & Jette Magilla
QVC
Issued: 1998
Value: N/E

EXCLUSIVE HARES

QVC, a leading retailer of Boyds exclusives, has offered many of the exclusive hares that have been produced. In addition, numerous pieces have been offered as specials to selected retailers, Dillard's and The San Francisco Music Box Company.

①

Allison Babbit
The San Francisco Music Box Company
♪ *I Only Have Eyes For You*
14" • #41-72141
Issued: 1998
Value: N/E

②

Alpine
Select Retailers
info unavailable
Value: N/E

③

Anissa
Select Retailers
Issued: 1998
Value: $40

④

Ashley
The San Francisco Music Box Company
♪ *Love Me Tender*
14" • #41-66847
Issued: 1997
Value: N/E

⑤

Bath & Body Works Snowbunny
Bath & Body Works
Issued: 1997
Value: N/E

⑥

Belle
Harry & David
8"
Issued: 1998
Value: N/E

⑦

Brittany
Dillard's
8" • #94711DL
Issued: 1997
Value: $30

⑧
PHOTO UNAVAILABLE

Caitlin
Dillard's
8"
Issued: 1997
Value: N/E

⑨

Chantanay
Select Retailers
info unavailable
Value: N/E

⑩

Demi
QVC
Issued: 1996
Value: $30

⑪

Dutch
Select Retailers
Issued: 1998
Value: N/E

⑫

Ellie
Select Retailers
Issued: 1998
Value: N/E

HARES
— EXCLUSIVE —

	Price Paid	Value Of My Collection
1.		
2.		
3.		
4.		
5.		
6.		
7.		
8.		
9.		
10.		
11.		
12.		
PENCIL TOTALS		

EXCLUSIVE HARES

① 	② 	③ 	④ 
Emily Babbit *QVC* Issued: 1998 **Value: N/E**	**Estelle** *Select Retailers* Issued: 1998 **Value: N/E**	**Floradora** *Select Retailers* Issued: 1998 **Value: N/E**	**Giselle &** **Monique de la Fleur** *QVC* Issued: 1998 **Value: N/E**
⑤ 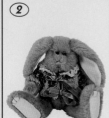	⑥ 	⑦ 	⑧ 
Grandma Babbit & **Elsinore** *QVC* Issued: 1996 **Value: $162**	**Grayling** *Select Retailers* Issued: 1998 **Value: $23**	**Gretchen** *Bon-Ton* *info unavailable* **Value: N/E**	**Gretchen** *Frederick Atkins* 8.5" Issued: 1998 **Value: N/E**

<table>
<tr><td colspan="2">

HARES

— EXCLUSIVE —

	Price Paid	Value Of My Collection
1.		
2.		
3.		
4.		
5.		
6.		
7.		
8.		
9.		
10.		
11.		
12.		
13.		
14.		

✏ PENCIL TOTALS

</td>
<td>

⑨

Harvey
QVC
Issued: 1995
Value: $55

⑫

New!

PHOTO
UNAVAILABLE

📷

Jenna Kathlean
Dillard's
11" • #94740DL
Issued: 1999
Value: $18

</td>
<td>

⑩

Heather
Dillard's
8" • #94709DL
Issued: 1997
Value: $27

⑬

Lacey V. Hare
QVC
Issued: 1998
Value: $28

</td>
<td>

⑪

Iris & Petunia
de la Hoppsack
QVC
Issued: 1998
Value: $35

⑭

Lady Harington
QVC
Issued: 1997
Value: $42

</td>
</tr>
</table>

(1)

Lady Harriwell
QVC
Issued: 1998
Value: $23

(2)

Lady Pembrooke
The San Francisco
Music Box Company
♪ *Music Box Dancer*
12" • #41-72647
Issued: 1998
Value: N/E

(3)

Lavinia V.
Hariweather
The San Francisco
Music Box Company
♪ *You Are My Sunshine*
10" • #41-72644
Issued: 1998
Value: N/E

(4)

Lindsey
Dillard's
8" • #94710DL
Issued: 1997
Value: $30

(5)

Mandy, Melissa &
Michael
QVC
Issued: 1998
Value: $22

(6)

New!

PHOTO
UNAVAILABLE

Meredith
Frederick Atkins
10"
Issued: 1999
Value: N/E

(7)

Ms. Magnolia,
Lauren & Elizabeth
QVC
Issued: 1997
Value: $105

(8)

Nanna O'Harea &
Audrey
QVC
Issued: 1998
Value: N/E

(9)

Natalie
Dillard's
14" • #94716DL
Issued: 1997
Value: N/E

(10)

Parker
Select Retailers
Issued: 1998
Value: $25

(11)

Pauline
Kirlin's
10"
Issued: 1997
Value: $43

(12)

Penelope
Select Retailers
10"
Issued: 1998
Value: N/E

(13)

Reno
Select Retailers
info unavailable
Value: N/E

(14)

Stamford
QVC
Issued: 1997
Value: $45

HARES
— EXCLUSIVE —

	Price Paid	Value Of My Collection
1.		
2.		
3.		
4.		
5.		
6.		
7.		
8.		
9.		
10.		
11.		
12.		
13.		
14.		

PENCIL TOTALS

EXCLUSIVE HARES

①

Stanford
QVC
info unavailable
Value: N/E

②

Zelda Fitzhare
*The San Francisco
Music Box Company*
♪ *Feelin' Groovy*
17" • #41-72643
Issued: 1998
Value: N/E

EXCLUSIVE LAMBS

For those who love plush lambs, the adorable "Abbey Ewe" and "Brianne" pieces were only available from select outlets. Both pieces were issued in recent years, with "Abbey Ewe" appearing in 1998 and "Brianne" in 1997.

③

Abbey Ewe
*The San Francisco
Music Box Company*
♪ *Mairzy Doats*
14" • #41-72648
Issued: 1998
Value: N/E

④

Brianne
Select Retailers
Issued: 1997
Value: $27

EXCLUSIVE LIONS

"Braden" and "Zack" roared into the Boyds exclusive category in 1997, competing with each other for the title of king of the Boyds jungle.

HARES
— EXCLUSIVE —

	Price Paid	Value Of My Collection
1.		
2.		

LAMBS
— EXCLUSIVE —

3.		
4.		

LIONS
— EXCLUSIVE —

5.		
6.		

MICE
— EXCLUSIVE —

7.		

✏ PENCIL TOTALS

⑤

Braden
Select Retailers
Issued: 1997
Value: N/E

⑥

Zack
QVC
Issued: 1997
Value: $34

EXCLUSIVE MICE

While some may say it's a "rat race out there," since the late 1990s only a few mice have been produced as exclusives.

⑦

**PHOTO
UNAVAILABLE**

**Colby &
Port S. Mouski**
QVC
6" & 6"
Value: N/E

①

Dick, Harry & Tom
QVC
Issued: 1997
Value: $30

②

Gouda & Edam
QVC
Issued: 1998
Value: $45

③

Havarti Chrismouse
GCC
#94864GCC
Issued: 1998
Value: $30

EXCLUSIVE MOOSE

Including "Eddie Bauer," a moose exclusive designed for the store of the same name, these elusive exclusives have been a hot item. As a result, it has been quite difficult for collectors to find these coveted characters.

④

Eddie Bauer
Eddie Bauer
Issued: 1994
Value: $40

⑤

Emily Ann
Lord & Taylor
17"
Issued: 1997
Value: $50

⑥

Magnus P. Mossfield
QVC
17"
Value: N/E

⑦

Manfred Von Merrymoose
GCC
#94581GCC
Issued: 1997
Value: $45

⑧

Maxine Von Hindenmoose
QVC
Issued: 1997
Value: $52

⑨

PHOTO UNAVAILABLE

Meeka
Select Retailers
info unavailable
Value: $60

⑩

Mookie
Select Retailers
info unavailable
Value: $40

⑪

Mortimer
Lord & Taylor
Issued: 1996
Value: N/E

MICE – EXCLUSIVE –		
	Price Paid	Value Of My Collection
1.		
2.		
3.		
MOOSE – EXCLUSIVE –		
4.		
5.		
6.		
7.		
8.		
9.		
10.		
11.		
PENCIL TOTALS		

EXCLUSIVE MICE/MOOSE

①

Mukluk
Select Retailers
Issued: 1995
Value: $60

EXCLUSIVE PIGS

These pigs love to hog the spotlight in stores and catalogs, including four pieces offered through Dillard's and QVC, among other outlets. "Big Pig, Little Pig" a set of two swine, is probably one of the most difficult exclusives for pig collectors to find, as it was only offered through Canadian retailers in 1998.

②

Baby Rosebud
Harry & David
Issued: 1996
Value: N/E

③

Big Pig, Little Pig
Canadian
12" & 9" • #BC94279
Issued: 1998
Value: $50

④

PHOTO UNAVAILABLE

Big Pig, Little Pig
Select Retailers
10" & 8"
Issued: 1998
Value: N/E

⑤

PHOTO UNAVAILABLE

Erin
Dillard's
8"
Issued: 1998
Value: N/E

⑥

G. Wilbur McSwine
QVC
8"
Issued: 1997
Value: $35

MOOSE
— EXCLUSIVE —

	Price Paid	Value Of My Collection
1.		

PIGS
— EXCLUSIVE —

2.		
3.		
4.		
5.		
6.		
7.		
8.		
9.		
10.		
11.		
12.		

PENCIL TOTALS

⑦

Kaitlin & Kendall McSwine
QVC
8" & 5"
Issued: 1998
Value: N/E

⑧

Katie
Select Retailers
info unavailable
Value: N/E

⑨

Katie O'Pigg
Dillard's
Issued: 1997
Value: $27

⑩

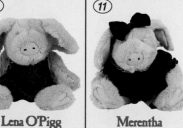

Lena O'Pigg
Dillard's
12" • #94706DL
Issued: 1997
Value: $33

⑪

Merentha
Dillard's
11" • #94727DL
Issued: 1997
Value: $40

⑫

Olympia
QVC
Issued: 1997
Value: N/E

①

Rosebud
Harry & David
8"
Issued: 1998
Value: N/E

②

Rosie O'Pigg
The San Francisco Music Box Company
♪ Second Hand Rose
11" • #41-72641
Issued: 1998
Value: N/E

EXCLUSIVE ORNAMENTS

Exclusive ornaments have been hanging around through the years, including a line of four famous fictional characters that were released in 1998, when Boyds worked in conjunction with Disney to produce ornaments featuring "Tigger," "Eeyore," "Piglet" and "Winnie The Pooh."

③

Annette Bearburg
Select Retailers
Issued: 1998
Value: $19

④

Arcturus & Aurora
QVC
5.5" & 5.5"
Issued: 1998
Value: N/E

⑤

Ardyth
GCC
#94861GCC
Issued: 1998
Value: $19

⑥

Ariel
QVC
Issued: 1996
Value: $45

⑦

Ariel
The San Francisco Music Box Company
♪ Jingle Bells
2" • #41-66894
Issued: 1997
Value: $35

⑧

Athena
Lord & Taylor
Issued: 1994
Value: N/E

⑨

Comet
Lord & Taylor
Issued: 1996
Value: N/E

⑩

Dolly & Jed
QVC
Issued: 1997
Value: N/E

⑪

Eeyore
Disney Catalog
Issued: 1998
Value: N/E

⑫

Fenton & Forest Silverton
QVC
Issued: 1998
Value: N/E

PIGS
— EXCLUSIVE —

	Price Paid	Value Of My Collection
1.		
2.		

ORNAMENTS
— EXCLUSIVE —

3.		
4.		
5.		
6.		
7.		
8.		
9.		
10.		
11.		
12.		
PENCIL TOTALS		

EXCLUSIVE PIGS/ORNAMENTS

①

Juliette
The San Francisco Music Box Company
♪ *Love Me Tender*
4" • #41-72646
Issued: 1998
Value: N/E

②

Lapis
QVC
Issued: 1996
Value: $35

③

Matilda
Lord & Taylor
Issued: 1994
Value: N/E

④

PHOTO UNAVAILABLE

Mrs. Bear In-The-Moon
Lord & Taylor
Issued: 1996
Value: N/E

⑤

Piglet
Disney Catalog
Issued: 1998
Value: N/E

⑥

Priscilla
Lord & Taylor
10"
Issued: 1997
Value: N/E

⑦

Snowbeary (set/3)
QVC
Issued: 1998
Value: N/E

⑧

Morley (set/3)
QVC
Issued: 1998
Value: N/E

ORNAMENTS
— EXCLUSIVE —

	Price Paid	Value Of My Collection
1.		
2.		
3.		
4.		
5.		
6.		
7.		
8.		
9.		
10.		

✏ PENCIL TOTALS

⑨

Tigger
Disney Catalog
Issued: 1998
Value: N/E

⑩

Winnie The Pooh
Disney Catalog
Issued: 1998
Value: N/E

Use these pages to record future Boyds releases.

FUTURE RELEASES	Series	Size	Item #	Issue Year	Status	Market Value	Price Paid	Value Of My Collection

PENCIL TOTALS

PRICE PAID	MARKET VALUE

FUTURE RELEASES

Use these pages to record future Boyds releases.

FUTURE RELEASES	Series	Size	Item #	Issue Year	Status	Market Value	Price Paid	Value Of My Collection

PENCIL TOTALS

PRICE PAID	MARKET VALUE

TOTAL VALUE OF MY COLLECTION

*Record the value of your collection here by adding the
pencil totals from the bottom of each value guide page.*

BOYDS PLUSH ANIMALS			BOYDS PLUSH ANIMALS		
Page Number	Price Paid	Market Value	Page Number	Price Paid	Market Value
Page 47			Page 86		
Page 48			Page 87		
Page 49			Page 88		
Page 50			Page 89		
Page 51			Page 90		
Page 52			Page 91		
Page 53			Page 92		
Page 54			Page 93		
Page 55			Page 94		
Page 56			Page 95		
Page 57			Page 96		
Page 58			Page 97		
Page 59			Page 98		
Page 60			Page 99		
Page 61			Page 100		
Page 62			Page 101		
Page 63			Page 102		
Page 64			Page 103		
Page 65			Page 104		
Page 66			Page 105		
Page 67			Page 106		
Page 68			Page 107		
Page 69			Page 108		
Page 70			Page 109		
Page 71			Page 110		
Page 72			Page 111		
Page 73			Page 112		
Page 74			Page 113		
Page 75			Page 114		
Page 76			Page 115		
Page 77			Page 116		
Page 78			Page 117		
Page 79			Page 118		
Page 80			Page 119		
Page 81			Page 120		
Page 82			Page 121		
Page 83			Page 122		
Page 84			Page 123		
Page 85			Page 124		
TOTAL			TOTAL		

TOTAL VALUE OF MY COLLECTION

Record the value of your collection here by adding the pencil totals from the bottom of each value guide page.

BOYDS PLUSH ANIMALS			BOYDS PLUSH ANIMALS		
Page Number	Price Paid	Market Value	Page Number	Price Paid	Market Value
Page 125			Page 160		
Page 126			Page 161		
Page 127			Page 162		
Page 128			Page 163		
Page 129			Page 164		
Page 130			Page 165		
Page 131			Page 166		
Page 132			Page 167		
Page 133			Page 168		
Page 134			Page 169		
Page 135			Page 170		
Page 136			Page 171		
Page 137			Page 172		
Page 138			Page 173		
Page 139			Page 174		
Page 140			Page 175		
Page 141			Page 176		
Page 142			Page 177		
Page 143			Page 178		
Page 144			Page 179		
Page 145			Page 180		
Page 146			Page 181		
Page 147			Page 182		
Page 148			Page 183		
Page 149			Page 184		
Page 150			Page 185		
Page 151			Page 186		
Page 152			Page 187		
Page 153			Page 188		
Page 154			Page 189		
Page 155			Page 190		
Page 156			Page 191		
Page 157			Page 192		
Page 158			Page 193		
Page 159			Page 194		
TOTAL			TOTAL		

GRAND TOTALS		
	PRICE PAID	MARKET VALUE

*W*hile any dedicated Boyds-a-holic will tell you that the real value of their Boyds animals comes from the love that the critters exude, it is impossible to ignore the fact that these creatures often increase in value as well. As new Boyds collectors surface, the demand for older and exclusive plush pieces is constantly increasing. This leads to the need for a secondary market, a place where collectors can obtain pieces that would normally be unattainable.

SECONDARY MARKET FACTORS

There are several factors that affect a piece's value on the secondary market.

1. CONDITION

Obviously, the pieces that command the highest values are those in the best condition.

2. RETIREMENT

Once a piece retires and slips out of the retail jungle, the chase is on. As a result, its value soars on the secondary market. (*For more information, see the Future Retirements section on page 42.*)

3. LIMITED EDITIONS

Produced for a limited amount of time or in a limited quantity, the most famous are the seasonal "Bailey And Friends" pieces (*for more information, see the Through The Years With Bailey And Friends section on page 9*) and *The Mohair Bears.*

4. PACKAGING

While most of the plush animals do not come in special packaging, *The Mohair Bears* come in special gift boxes. Like most collectibles, a piece that is missing its box will decrease in value on the secondary market.

BOYDS ON THE WEB

One of the fastest-growing and easiest ways to access the secondary market is by logging onto the Internet. Several sites have been dedicated to the lovable Boyds creatures, including chat rooms, which serve as a meeting ground for collectors, who often boast of forming lasting friendships with one another through these means. Auction sites and bulletin boards have become a quick and easy way to buy and sell pieces without leaving home.

OTHER RESOURCES

For a more personal venture into the secondary market, the best place to start is with your local retailer. While they are not usually active in the secondary market themselves, they are often able to provide great direction as to where to go. Secondary market exchange services are another popular option for buying and selling collectibles. The exchange, which often requires a subscription and charges a brokerage fee, provides a listing of pieces for sale. See CheckerBee Publishing's Boyds Bears & Friends™ Collector's Value Guide™ (which features Boyds resin figurines) for a comprehensive listing of Boyds exchanges, dealers and newsletters.

Keep in mind that the market is constantly fluctuating and collectors who are in it solely for the financial return will most likely be disappointed. Bear hunting should be about the thrill of the chase and the excitement that comes from the capture!

$\mathcal{A}$s every Boyds plush animal is hand-crafted, each one has its own slightly unique characteristics. While many of these are subtle, collectors will occasionally discover more obvious differences. These differences are called variations and generally result from one of two circumstances: either human error or an intended alteration of the original design or pattern. And although many minor variations can occur, the majority of variations in the Boyds plush line fall into the following categories: clothing changes, eye changes, fur changes, pattern changes and non-physical changes.

WHAT TO WEAR

We all know that clothes make the man, but it's true that they make the plush animal too. "Helmut," the moose sported a spiffy green sweater for a short time until he discovered that red was more his color. And in the spring of 1994, poor "Edmund" just couldn't decide if he wanted to wear navy or black.

IT'S ALL IN THE EYES

We often wish to see the world through a different pair of eyes and many Boyds cats have been able to do just that. "Millicent P. Pussytoes" is one among many who was seeing green for a while, as well as a more yellow shade.

A NEW COAT

Sometimes it's hard to keep these critters out of the hair dye – after all, we all need a change once in a while. One example of this variation is the lovely "Corinna" who has sported different shades of brown fur throughout her lifespan.

A BIT OF COSMETICS

Over the years, Boyds plush animals have gotten a face-lift of sorts. For example, "Abercrombie B. Beanster" enters this spring season with the new look for the *J.B. Bean & Associates*. His design features larger ears and longer arms, as well as legs that are a bit shorter and feet that show some growth.

Others, such as "Avery B. Bean," decided that they might be giving a less-than-sophisticated impression with their open mouths and protruding tongues and newer styles take a more closed-mouth stance.

NOT JUST SKIN DEEP

Many of the Boyds characters have also undergone non-physical changes. "Father Krismoose" decided to take on the less formal name of "Kris Moose" while "Eddie Beanbauer" decided that maybe a more original name might be better and changed it to "Eddie Beanberger," with his companion "Teddy Beanbauer" making a similar decision.

An astute collector will notice that throughout the years, according to catalogs, these characters' item numbers and sizes (which may just be the result of a different style of measuring) change over the years. In rare cases, so do names (as with "Alec," who can be found as "Alex" on some Boyds literature, and "Diana," who is also known as "Elizabeth").

ALL FUN AND GAMES

Remember that while it is always exciting to discover a variation, there is no guarantee that the change will be highly recognized or gain significant value on the secondary market.

*W*hen insuring your collection, there are three major points to consider:

1. KNOW YOUR COVERAGE: Collectibles are typically included in homeowner's or renter's insurance policies. Ask your agent if your policy covers fire, theft, floods, hurricanes, earthquakes and damage or breakage from routine handling. Also, ask if your policy covers claims at "current replacement value" – the amount it would cost to replace items if they were damaged, lost or stolen. This is extremely important since the secondary market value of some pieces may well exceed their original retail price.

2. DOCUMENT YOUR COLLECTION: In the event of a loss, you will need a record of the contents and value of your collection. Ask your insurance agent what information is acceptable. Keep receipts and an inventory of your collection in a different location, such as a safe deposit box. Include the purchase date, price paid, size, issue year, edition limit/number, special markings and secondary market value for each piece. Photographs and video footage with close-up views of each piece, including tags, boxes and signatures, are good back-ups.

3. WEIGH THE RISK: To determine the coverage you need, calculate how much it would cost to replace your collection and compare it to the total amount your current policy would pay. To insure your collection for a specific dollar amount, ask your agent about adding a Personal Articles Floater or a Fine Arts Floater or "rider" to your policy, or insuring your collection under a separate policy. As with all insurance, you must weigh the risk of loss against the cost of additional coverage.

Production

PRODUCTION

A design is born when Gary Lowenthal first sketches out the ideas that come into his mind. When the sketch is complete and Lowenthal is satisfied with how it looks (a design may go through several revisions), he will begin the piece's production by enlisting the talents of a seamstress.

Once in the seamstress' hand, the piece comes to life. Production begins when a pattern is cut either by hand or machine, mostly depending on the complexity of the design.

Once the pattern has been cut, the piece is stitched together by hand. Room is left to add stuffing and once the desired "feel" is achieved, the piece receives a few more stitches and is ready for its final touches.

Next, the paws, nose and mouth are added to the piece. Again, this is all done by hand; giving each piece its own unique look.

PACKAGING

The animals arrive at stores packed in bags, with the exception of *The Mohair Bears*, which are packed in individual gift boxes. Most of the animals come with a tag,which often features the hand-written name of the animal.

PRICING

While the plush animals vary in cost between $6 and $50, most can found between the range of $15 and $25.

Display Tips

*F*inding new and original ways of displaying your Boyds pieces can be just as much fun as shopping for them! You can make your display as simple or as extravagant as you wish. A simple series of shelves grouped to show off your collection can be effective (or add a little whimsy to your favorite piece of household furniture, such as an old dresser – you never know where these characters might like to hang out). Or, if you wish, you can use miniatures, as well as Boyds accessories, to create different scenarios that you can update frequently to match the season or your changing moods. Whatever you decide, there is a wide variety of options available for those who want to bring the wilds of the Boyds collection into their home. To help you get started, here's a couple of ideas:

Tea Time – Treat your favorite animals to their very own place to have some fun (and trade some gossip)! Boyds makes plenty of bear and hare-sized furniture and accessories and miniature tea sets are available through most toy or craft stores. Add some flowers and a few doilies doubling as tablecloths and you've got yourself the perfect afternoon outing. Just don't forget that bears LOVE honey in their tea, while cats purr-fer milk!

Roadside Stand – Why not let your bears and hares earn a little spending money by setting up their very own business? Although retired, Boyds has put out several concession stands perfect for selling pumpkins, apples and of course, everyone's favorite . . . honey! A variety of pumpkins, pies and gourds are available through Boyds and enhance these displays nicely. You can find miniature trees at a hobby shop and changing the season of the scene is as easy as changing the type of tree you use. Scatter dried leaves or hay and add a few well-placed sale signs for excellent finishing touches.

School Days – As school gets back into session, dress your bears in their favorite sweaters and scholarly glasses to prepare them for the new year in style. Set up a series of miniature desks arranged around a small blackboard and add some accent accessories that can be found at your local craft store such as bear-sized books, pencils and lunch boxes. Many of your "students" can be posed holding an apple for the teacher, while others may prefer to sit on the sidelines, book in hand, studying for an upcoming test.

Let's Get Cooking – "Aunt Becky Bearchild" keeps one eye on her little pal who is baking for the first time with "Bailey's Cast Iron Cook Stove." A number of great accessories are available from your favorite Boyds retailer for this display and you can set up a cozy nook with "Bailey's Parisian Bistro Table With Two Chairs" so your friends can sit down and enjoy their meal, too!

'Tis The Season – Attach (with wire) plush pieces, along with your Boyds ornaments to create a dazzling display tree!

*O*ver the years, Boyds accessories have become nearly as popular as the animals for which they were made. From sweaters to schooners, Boyds now makes a wide variety of products to make sure that your cuddly friends have everything they need to live life to its fullest. Keep in mind that some of the products listed below may have retired and, therefore, are harder to find!

Accessories

THE BEAR ESSENTIALS

While several Boyds critters arrive wearing their Sunday best, others come "bear" naked. So, whether shopping for a complete wardrobe or just something to wear while their favorite outfit is in the laundry, your animals can find several items to make them the best dressed creatures on the block.

Glasses – Have you noticed any of your plush companions squinting lately? Maybe a pair of stylish glasses will help! Whether your bear really needs them or just wants to achieve that scholarly look, Boyds makes glasses for every taste. So, depending on their mood, your animals can either impersonate their favorite musician with the "Garcia" specs or can achieve a more serious look with the "Roosevelt" frames.

Sweaters – When it gets chilly outside, bundle up your loved ones in warm Boyds pullovers and cardigans. From the sweaters with hearts for Valentine's Day, to the Christmas-inspired knits perfect for the holiday season, you can be sure your critters will be warm all year round!

Hats – When these lovable little creatures get head colds, they can become "unbearable!" So, to avoid any problems, protect these little guys with custom-made hats (often complete with ear holes) before they head outside!

AROUND THE HOUSE

While these furry little creatures really appreciate being a part of your home, everything's just a little too big for them! Make them feel more at home with some furniture of their own. What bear or hare wouldn't love to settle down onto his own comfy, custom made "Rutherford's Plaid Cub Chair & Ottoman" while watching TV with your family? And with a full array of appliances from "Aunt Becky's Ol' Fashion Iron" to "Bailey's Cast Iron Cook Stove," maybe you'll be lucky enough to come home and find your clothes for the upcoming week all ironed as well as a tasty treat prepared by your furry friends!

AT WORK AND AT PLAY

Are your animals getting cabin fever? Boyds has a number of accessories to keep them active outdoors while the weather is nice. While the older bears keep busy running a concession stands, the little ones can play with their "Wooden Rowboats" (which come in red, green or blue). And when it's time to plant your garden, your Boyds friends can help you with "Lucy's Harvest Wheelbarrow" while you do the planting.

H.M.S. BOYDS

A PICNIC

A number of baskets are available from Boyds, including "Auntie Em's Rattan Picnic Baskets," which are perfect for those lazy summer days spent at the lake. And as pictures are worth a thousand words, let your critters save the memory of the day with "McNibble's Saycheez Camera."

BED TIME

After a long hard day, your plush animals can snuggle up in their "Bear Paw Lodge Bunk Bed." "Paxton's Lone Star Quilt" and "Katie's Floral Quilt" will be the perfect snuggling companions for those long winter nights.

FOR THE OWNERS

What do you get for the Boyds fanatic who seems to have everything? Besides the plush and resin collections, Boyds has produced a number of other products that are spilling into every facet of everyday life and that are just as endearing.

Kitchenware – In 1997, Gary produced a line called Bearware Potteryworks that feature those lovable Boyds bears on ceramic kitchen accessories. The line consists of cookie jars and salt and pepper shakers, all designed in the 1940's style glossy finish. Also available for your kitchen (or den, or office) are a wide variety of Boyds mugs, perfect for holding a plethora of drinks.

Wearable Boyds – Boyds has created an assortment of adorably patterned sweatshirts and T-shirts so you can show off your Boyds no matter what the weather! In addition, baseball hats, with or without ears, featuring the Boyds company logo are available for bear enthusiasts. And to satisfy that gnawing case of ear envy, The Boyds Collection Ltd. finally made those fashionable furry bear ears often seen on the Head Bean Hisself available to collectors.

Home Decor – All those proud to be a "Bearmerican" can show their devotion with a Boyds flag. While the majority of the flag collection has been retired, some may still be hanging around.

An assortment of picture frames and votive holders are available as part of the resin line that make great decorative accents to your home. An exciting addition in the way of home decor is the *Le Bearmoge*™ Collection which features your favorite resin characters atop porcelain boxes. And each piece has its own little surprise inside.

There is something for almost everyone and almost every occasion from The Boyds Collection Ltd.

LICENSED PRODUCTS

The growing demand for "MORE, MORE, MORE!" Boyds products brought about The Boyds Collection Ltd.'s decision to begin licensing their images to a variety of different companies.

In 1997, Sunrise, a leading greeting card manufacturer, was named the official licensee of Boyds cards, the first of the Boyds licensed products. Since then, the collection has grown to include gift wrap, bags, invitations, note pads, journals and stationery. Most recently, the company began producing Boyds scrapbook kits; which include stationery, paper frames and an assortment of adorable Boyds stickers.

Manual Woodworkers & Weavers produces a full line of woven articles featuring the colorful Boyds family. Boyds lovers can cuddle up to a variety of Boyds afghans, all produced in soft chenille for ultimate comfort. The company also designs many other products with the famous friendly faces, including pillows, wall hangings and cloth calendars.

To keep Boyds fans in touch with their creative sides, the folks at Uptown Rubber Stamps recently began distribution on a new line of stamps. Included with each stamping kit is a "how-to" brochure that will help even novice stampers create their very own beautiful, personalized products.

So, no matter what you, or your bear, needs, Boyds is sure to supply it; from accessories for the well-dressed animal to critter-sized kitchens, as well as Boyds-themed human sized ones. For more information on the newest Boyds products, watch *The Boyds Bear Retail Inquirer* and to see what is currently available, contact your local retailer.

GLOSSARY

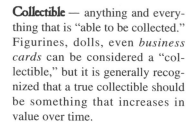

Collectible — anything and everything that is "able to be collected." Figurines, dolls, even *business cards* can be considered a "collectible," but it is generally recognized that a true collectible should be something that increases in value over time.

Exchange — a secondary market service that lists pieces that collectors wish to buy or sell. The exchange works as a middleman and may require a commission.

Exclusive — a plush animal made especially for, and available only through, a specific store, buying group or wholesaler.

International Collectible Exposition — a national collectible show held annually in June in Rosemont, Illinois and in April alternating between Long Beach, California (1999) and Edison, New Jersey (2000).

Jointed — describes a piece whose arms, legs or head move.

Launch — the debut of a piece on the home shopping channel QVC. These pieces are usually released to stores in the following months.

Limited Edition (LE) — a piece scheduled for a predetermined production quantity or time period.

Mint Condition — a piece offered on the secondary market that is in like-new condition.

Primary Market — the conventional collectibles purchasing process in which collectors buy directly from dealers at retail price.

Retired — a piece that is taken out of production, never to be made again. This is usually followed by a scarcity of the piece and an increase in value on the secondary market.

Secondary Market — the source for buying and selling collectibles according to basic supply-and-demand principles ("pay what the market will bear"). Popular pieces that are sold out or have been retired can appreciate in value far above the original issue price. Pieces are sold through newspaper ads, collector newsletters, the Internet and "swap & sells" at collector gatherings.

Sudden Death Retirement — the sudden, "unplanned" removal of a piece from production (at the discretion of the "Head Bean"). Pieces designated as sudden death retirements are retired as soon as the stock runs out. Typically, Boyds retirements are announced in advance.

Variations — pieces that have color, design or printed text changes from the "original" piece, whether intentional or not. Some are minor changes, while some are important enough to affect the piece's value on the secondary market.

BEARFINDER – ALPHABETICAL INDEX

BEARFINDER – ALPHABETICAL INDEX

215

BEARFINDER – ALPHABETICAL INDEX

ACKNOWLEDGEMENTS

CheckerBee Publishing would like to extend a special thanks to Harry & Millie Croft, Suzie Hocker and Capt'n Ron & Kristy Northman. Also thanks to Lori Bergland, Linda Brand, Kelly Brannen, Denise Casemier, Julie Christensen, Linda Cross, Brenda Fry, Melissa Gabbard, Lynn Hamilton, Doris Hoffman, Kim Houston, Teddy Huppert, Sally Jechura, Shari Martin, Annmarie Pearlstein, Dave & Linda Reinhart, Kristin Sheaffer, Mark & Jean Ann Sovereign, Linda Stratton, Jo Ann Teresi and Diana Webb. Many thanks to the great people at The Boyds Collection Ltd.

Boyds Bears & Friends™
presents the

1999 F.o.B. Membership

Plant with Hope...Grow with Love...Bloom with Joy!

The Loyal Order of
Friends of Boyds™

This is it!

This is how you become a

Genuine "Bloomin' F.o.B!"

That's an Official 1999 Member of...

The Loyal Order of
Friends of Boyds™

(F.o.Bs for Short!)

A Slightly Off-Center Collector's Club
for people who still believe in...
BEARS AND HARES YOU CAN TRUST™

And have we got a story for you, turn the page ☞

H ere it iz...yer very own, extra
special Membership Application!

And you don't have to wait until your anniversary date
(the date you joined the Club) to renew!

CHECK ONE: ❑ Current Member ID# _____
❑ New Member

NAME _____

ADDRESS _____

CITY _____

STATE _____ ZIP CODE _____

DAYTIME PHONE (_____) _____

DATE OF BIRTH *(year optional)* _____

❑ YES, I want to be a "Bloomin' F.o.B." for $32.⁵⁰
(PA residents with 6% sales tax = $34.45)

❑ Make it a 2-Year Membership instead
(Good thru 2000!), just **$63.00** _____
(PA residents with 6% sales tax = $66.78)

❑ Add The Official F.o.B. Mug $7.⁵⁰
(PA residents with 6% sales tax = $7.95)

GRAND TOTAL _____

FORM OF PAYMENT: ❑ Check ❑ Money Order

MAKE PAYABLE TO: The Boyds Collection Ltd.®
P.O. Box 4386 F.o.B. Dept.
Gettysburg, PA 17325-4386

CREDIT CARD CHOICE: ❑ Master Card ❑ Visa

CREDIT CARD NUMBER: Exp. Date ___/___/___

AUTHORIZED SIGNATURE:

_____

*(Authorized signature must accompany charge request.
Card will be processed at time of shipment.)*

I understand that my membership kit will be shipped 12 to 16 weeks
following receipt of this application at The Boyds Collection.
Offer Expires December 31, 1999

WHO IS YOUR RETAILER?
(you know the place where you purchase your Boyds stuff)

Name _____ ID# _____

City _____ State _____ Zip _____

Once upon a time in the Land of Boyds...

...lived Flora Mae Berriweather and her daughter Blossum. Flora was famous for her Green Thumb...she seemed to win all of the Blue Ribbons in Gardening at the County Fair. Blossum wanted to plant a garden and be just like her Mom!

🐾 One day Flora Mae said, "Blossum, I have some special seeds for your Garden." And she told Blossum the secrets of growing a good garden. She said, "If you think you <u>can</u> do something, you <u>will</u> be able to do it. So remember...**Plant with Hope**, (the first secret) and see what happens!"

🐾 So Blossum found a sunny spot for planting...and soon a green shoot appeared. Every day she applied the second secret...watered it & talked to it, and her little plant **Grew with Love**...and *grew*, and GREW into a Giant Sunflower twice as tall as Blossum herself! Flora Mae proudly watched her daughter, and one summer day she said, "Blossum, get your Sunflower ready for the judging at tomorrow's County Fair!"

🐾 Well, when ol' Judge Griz (who moonlights as a County Fair Judge, you know) came to Blossum's Sunflower, he saw right away that it deserved the Blue Ribbon...and the only thing bigger & brighter than that bloomin' Sunflower was the smile on Blossum's face as she learned the final secret...**Bloom with Joy!**

◆◆◆

So, to remind you to "**Plant with Hope...Grow with Love...Bloom with Joy!**", in <u>anything</u> you do...here's our 1999 Club Kit. Reward or encourage yourself or a Special Someone with our "Blossum" and "Flora Mae" pieces!

🐾 **Flora Mae Berriweather...Grow with Love!** She's a Bee-you-ti-ful 6" bear dressed in a buttercup yellow handknit cardigan sweater & matching sunny yellow felt hat complete with a big ol' Sunflower on the front. (Aunt Mabel, eat your heart out!)

🐾 **"Blossum B. Berriweather... Bloom with Joy!"** Exclusive Bearstone This one's a dandy! Blossum is standing under her prize winning sunflower which has grown to a whopping 4¼" high (well, that's a <u>Giant</u> in Boyds Bearstone Land!)

🐾 Genuine "Bloomin' F.o.B." Sunflower Seed Packet! This is sooo luverly, if we do say so ourselves. The custom-designed Sunflower Seed Packet is 'specially created only for "Bloomin' F.o.B.s." And yes, there really <u>are</u> genuine Sunflower seeds in there!

🐾 A Year's Subscription to the F.o.B. Inquirer - The only newspaper written by The Head Bean Hisself! And guess what? In response to Popular Demand by our current F.o.Bs (see...we do listen!) we will Double our number of Issues. Okay...that means we're going from 2 issues per year to 4 - but that's as fast as The Head Bean can write!

All This And More...

🐾 "Bloomin' F.o.B." 1999 Bearstone Pin, The Boyds Bears & Friends Dealer Directory, A Boyds Bears & Friends Product List...

Prices Rising??? Not Here at Boyds...The Head Bean says Membership is **Still Only $32.50!**

◆◆◆

But Wait! We're slaving away to bring you Extra Special Opportunities too...and they're available only to our 1999 Club Members!

First...The chance to buy the new first-ever **1999 Official F.o.B. Mug!** Yep! That's Right! This exclusive Members Only Piece features some of the custom artwork of the seed packet (and more!) wrapped around a luverly mug. And it's a lot neater than trying to drink your coffee from that seed packet to proclaim you're a "Bloomin' F.o.B."!

Second...our exclusive Members Only Plush Bears, **Hope, Love and Joy** and our Bearstone piece, **Sunny and Sally**...that you can order from your favorite B.B. & F. Retailer...this year!